THE
EROSION
OF
OXFORD

THE EROSION OF OXFORD

James Stevens Curl

Oxford Illustrated Press 1977

PHOTOGRAPHIC ACKNOWLEDGEMENTS

All photographs not credited below have been taken by the author

Oxford County Libraries
Chapter One: figs. 3, 7, 8, 11-13, 16-19, 21, 23-6, 28, 30, 51, 52
Chapter Two: figs. 5, 10, 11, 17
Chapter Three: figs. 3, 9, 20, 22, 29, 35, 36, 38
Chapter Five: figs. 28, 29
Chapter Six: fig. 2
Epilogue: fig. 8

Ken Smith
Chapter One: fig. 20
Chapter Three: figs. 10, 14, 39
Chapter Four: fig. 17
Chapter Five: figs. 15-17
Chapter Six: figs. 10, 16
Chapter Seven: figs. 1, 2, 4
Chapter Eight: fig. 4
Epilogue: fig. 1

Oxford Architects' Partnership
Chapter One: fig. 48

Oxford Mail & Times
Chapter One: figs. 34-6, 38, 39, 41, 44, 49, 50
Chapter Two: fig. 21
Chapter Six: fig. 6

Rodney C. Roach
Chapter One: figs. 4, 5, 22
Chapter Three: fig. 6
Chapter Seven: figs. 11-18

Thomas Rayson Partnership
Chapter Three: figs. 5, 7, 8

Oxford Illustrated Press Ltd, Shelley Close, Headington, Oxford

Set by Parchments in the City of Oxford
Film by Knight Publishing Ltd
Printed by Blackwells in the City of Oxford
ISBN 0 902280 40 6

Contents

for

A. H. Buck

with
affection and gratitude

Introduction

'Oxford is on the whole more
attractive than Cambridge to the
ordinary visitor; and the traveller is
therefore recommended to visit
Cambridge first, or to omit it
altogether if he cannot visit both.'

Carl Baedeker (1801–1859)

The editorial in the *Oxford Mail* on 21 February 1968 read as follows:

Ugliness is taken too much for granted. This is the lesson of Adytum's[1] series on the Erosion of Oxford, although it applies all over the country.

In Oxford's suburbs there are examples of appalling dreariness and — on the outskirts — of scruffiness. North Oxford shows how large trees can give variety to the scene. Adytum's suggestion of a tree-planting campaign elsewhere is to the point.

Oxford City Council provided some of the object lessons. There is the road lay-out of Rose Hill which ignores the view. Blackbird Leys — which should be the council's showpiece — has at its centre a jumble of unrelated buildings which suggest that the council did not know where it was going when it began.

The lessons must be learned in rebuilding St. Ebbe's. Already the council has been driven — because of Mr. Crossman's[2] indecision — to build roads with no clear idea how the spaces created between them[3] are to be filled. Roads and buildings should be designed together. The council must decide priorities for the use of land in St. Ebbe's and get a complete scheme drawn up before any more piece-meal decisions are taken.

This noted the end of the first series of articles on the Erosion of Oxford. When the first of the 'Adytum' articles was published in the *Oxford Mail* on 25 October 1968, the 'environmental lobby' was relatively muted compared with the situation of the mid-seventies. Those of us who cared for the architectural values of the past were very much in a minority, while roads, traffic, motor cars, and non-traditional architecture were all accepted as essential aspects of 'progressive' thought. All that has now changed and even the 'Modern Movement' in Architecture is no longer quite respectable.

The Oxford Civic Society, of which I was the first Chairman, was formed because a few citizens of Oxford became very worried by the erosion of the historic city's character by the systematic destruction of the minor architecture and by the appalling scale of the road plans proposed. The campaigns of the Civic Society, though time-consuming, exhausting, and, at times, apparently hopeless, eventually bore fruit: no 'inner relief road' has so far been built to disrupt five major communities and further overload the hard-pressed ratepayers; a traffic management scheme has been partially implemented, with some pedestrianisation; and the authorities are erecting period Windsor lanterns within certain areas of outstanding character.

On 2 April 1970 the *Oxford Mail* reported the Civic Society's objections to the new road network proposed by the city's consultants.

When inner relief roads were first proposed for Oxford, they were the accepted solution to the problems of movement within a city. Now it is becoming recognised that the unrestricted use of the car in cities destroys environment and is socially damaging. Oxford, one of our most ancient cities as well as the home of a great university, deserves a more imaginative solution to its problems than the proposed plan.

The Society recommended that the rôle of public transport should be re-examined, with the object of eliminating commuter traffic within the city boundary, and reducing numbers of other cars to a minimum. Within a week, on 9 April 1970, the Editorial of the *Oxford Mail* was questioning the Civic Society's stand, but subsequent events (the energy crisis, oil prices, economic decline, and a probable fall in car ownership) have more than justified the views of the Civic Society.

The publication *Let's LIVE in Oxford* put the Civic Society on the map, and cogently argued for the restriction of the motor car, while urging that one of the most beautiful and famous cities in Europe had to be saved from the sure destruction entailed in building urban motorways. With pithy wit, the Society declared that it would be a pity if 'Oxford, the traditional home of lost causes, supports what is destined to be perhaps the biggest lost cause of all — the accommodation of the car in towns.'

Oxford is not just the University area with its magnificent historic buildings. It consists of many suburbs and established communities, each with its own character. Many of these suburbs have ancient centres, once hamlets or small villages, now swallowed up within the urban mass, but most retaining a strong sense of place.

I have been able to include some contrasting pictures, showing how certain parts of the city have changed. An interesting record of 'before' and 'after' photographs may be found in *Oxford Past and Present*, compiled by C. W. Judge, and published by the Oxford Illustrated Press in 1970. This book contained photographs from the Harry Minn Collection, some items of which are contained in the present work. Another fascinating glimpse of Victorian Oxford may be found in *Henry Taunt of Oxford. A Victorian Photographer*, by Malcolm Graham, also published by the Oxford Illustrated Press, this time in 1973. Both the Bodleian and County Libraries contain a mine of splendid historical pictorial material, only a sample of which it is possible to reproduce.

The purpose of this book is to celebrate Oxford and to deplore what has happened to it, while at the same time to suggest some positive steps which might be taken to conserve and enhance what is left. It is at once an elegy, a cry of pain, and an exasperated, affectionate remembrance of many years of residence in that city. Readers will look in vain for a detailed inventory of the grander buildings; others have carried out that task admirably. This book will look at the humbler aspects of the urban fabric and will concentrate on the everyday things that ordinary people see, or do not see, depending on their visual awareness. It is hoped that this book will encourage people to use their eyes and their critical faculties in order to understand the terrible damage that is daily being inflicted on a national treasure. The grander University buildings, we trust, can look after themselves for the time being, because they, at least, are officially recognised as being of importance.

I am indebted to Mr. Mark Barrington-Ward and the proprietors of the *Oxford Mail* for permission to reproduce some photographs and other material previously published; to the Librarian and Staff of the Oxford County Libraries for help in providing historical material; to Mr. and Mrs. Gerard L'Estrange Turner for general encouragement; to Professor Edmund W. Gilbert for invaluable help; to Mr. Richard Blackwell who persuaded me to write this book; to Mr. Rodney Roach who helped me quickly and efficiently, as always, with the processing of my photographs; to Mr. Thomas Braun who spurred me on; to Mr. Christopher Rayson and his late father for their help; to Mr. A. H. Buck who not only allowed me to dedicate this book to him but who nobly and bravely read the proofs for me; to Mr. and Mrs. K. Lichtenstein, who first showed me the 'hidden mysteries of Oxford', and who gave me many years of friendship and considerable kindnesses; to Mrs. Penelope Jessel who gave me hospitality and much help; to Mr. Michael Drew for finding illustrations; and to Miss Helen Logan who typed the book from an inelegant manuscript.

James Stevens Curl
1975

---

[1] *Adytum:* The author's pseudonym. The term means the innermost part of a temple, or the secret shrine from which oracles were delivered.
[2] The late Richard Crossman, formerly Minister of Housing and Local Government.
[3] Known as SLOAP (Space Left Over After Planning).

1

The City of Oxford

'A kind of terror always falls upon
me as I near it . . . indignation at
wanton or rash changes mingles
anxiously in me with all that I
remember I have lost since I was a
lad and dwelling there.'

William Morris writing to
Georgiana Burne-Jones

Fig. 1: *Part of the old city wall in the grounds of New College*
Fig. 2: *The Church of St. Peter-in-the-East, now the library of St. Edmund Hall*

Oxford is centrally placed in the Upper Thames basin. It is also situated centrally in the South Midlands — South of England, and is placed almost equidistant (c. 100 km) from London, Bristol, Southampton, and Birmingham. Some geographers have therefore argued as if Oxford is within the London or West Midland region of England, while others have given Oxford its own region. Oxford is the service centre for an area of approximately 2,200 km^2 with a population of about 350,000. The population of the city is about 108,000.

Oxford is situated at the junction of the rivers Thames and the Cherwell. There was a bridge over the Cherwell by the beginning of the eleventh century, and during the twelfth, a causeway, incorporating a bridge over the Thames, was built to the south. Another causeway was formed during the sixteenth century and this bridged the many channels of the Thames to the west.

The city lies in the centre of a low-lying plain between the Cots-wolds in the north and the Berkshire Downs and Chilterns on the south and east. From Carfax tower, Oxford seems to lie at the bottom of a saucer-shaped depression surrounded by low-lying hills about 110 m in height.

The mediaeval city was about 1 km long from west to east and about 600 m wide from north to south. It was surrounded by walls, portions of which survive, and a castle dominated the low-lying lands to the west. The total area of the city within the walls was about 38 hectares. Pre-Conquest defences were strengthened after 1066, and the Castle and Mound were built in 1071. Since Oxford was a port, the Castle commanded the landing-places, and from the Castle routes led west towards the Saxon village of North Hinksey over four fords across the branches of the Thames. It may have been from one of those fords that the city derived its name. The West Gate was near the Castle, and the East Gate was some 274 m west of the Cherwell and Magdalen Bridge on the line of the High Street. Other gates were the South Gate, about 100 m north of the Thames at Folly Bridge at the end of Fish Street (now St. Aldate's), the North Gate at the end of North Gate Street (now Cornmarket) by St. Michael's Church and Smith Gate at the north end of Cat Street (now pretentiously named Catte Street) near the junction with Holywell.

While there may have been ancient settlements on the site, Oxford's rise as an important place dates from the ninth century. The area of the mediaeval city was apparently established by the year 1000, although most of the fabric of the surviving city wall dates from the latter half of the fourteenth century. The most complete parts of the wall are in the grounds of New College, and are complete with bastions, battlements, and steps (fig. 1). The South Gate was demolished by Cardinal Wolsey when the college of Christ Church was built; the West Gate was pulled down at the end of the sixteenth century; and the North and East Gates were demolished in the latter half of the eighteenth century. There were churches dedicated to St. Michael at both the North and South Gates, and churches dedicated to St. Peter stood near the West and East Gates. The Church of St. Peter-in-the-East still stands, though today it is a library for the College of St. Edmund Hall (fig. 2).

There were many churches in mediaeval Oxford. Dedications included: St. Budoc (demolished); St. Ebbe (partly twelfth and thirteenth century, though mostly nineteenth century, with work by G. E. Street);

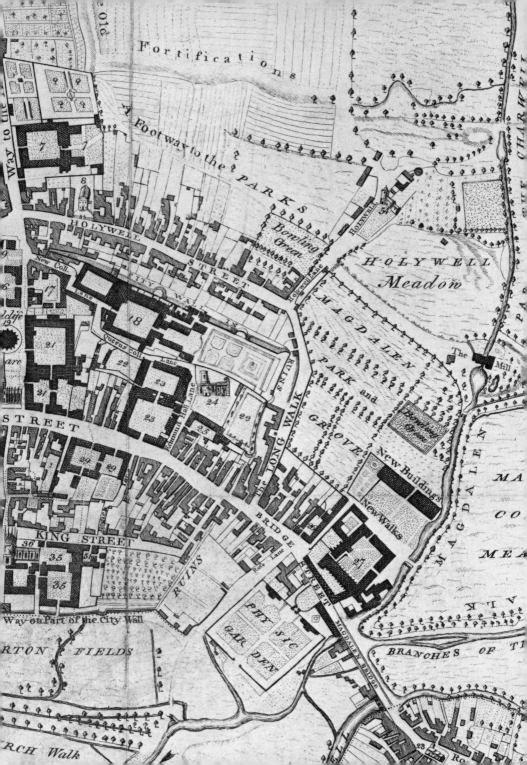

Fig. 3: Carfax, showing the old Church of St. Martin being demolished in 1896.

Facing page: fig. 4 The Saxon tower of St. Michael at the North Gate

Overleaf: The Longmate map of Oxford, 1773

St. Martin (situated at Carfax but with only the tower remaining, as the
church was demolished in 1896 for road-widening purposes [fig. 3]); St.
Aldate (still standing, but very much over-restored by J. T. Christopher
in 1862—74); St. Michael (the church at the South Gate has been
demolished, but that of the North Gate still stands [fig. 4]. The tower
is late Anglo-Saxon, of about 1000, and the mediaeval church body
was largely rebuilt in Victorian and modern times); St. Mildred
(demolished); All Saints (rebuilt in 1706—8 by Dean Aldrich in a
Classical manner, and joined with the dedication of St. Martin in 1896,
it is now the library of Lincoln College); St. Peter (St. Peter-le-Bailey,
now moved to a different site as the chapel of St. Peter's College and
designed in 1874 by Basil Champneys, and also St. Peter-in-the-East,
perhaps the finest mediaeval church in Oxford, with a Norman crypt);
St. Mary (the Parish Church of Oxford, with its spectacular fourteenth-
century spire); Holy Trinity (at the East Gate now demolished); St.
John (now Merton College Chapel); St. Frideswide (now Christ Church
Cathedral); and St. Edward the Martyr (demolished). There were other
dedications immediately outside the walls, including St. Giles, St. Mary
Magdalen, and others.

The basic street pattern is cruciform, with the extremities of the
cross at the four main gates. The junction of the four main ways is
called Carfax, from the Middle English *carfuks*, derived from the Latin

6

Fig. 5: Villas in Banbury Road looking north, showing the substantial houses and mature planting.

quadrifurcus, meaning four-forked. The fairly regular rectangular blocks between the main streets and the walls probably had a basis in the subdivision into plots for letting and building, and is a common mediaeval pattern. The present street plan within the old walled city is almost the same as it was in the thirteenth century with the exception of the late eighteenth-century changes when New Road was driven from Great Bailey (Queen Street) to Botley Road, and when the Westgate development was built over part of the site of the wall. During the eighteenth century Oxford gradually expanded, and during Victorian times whole new suburbs were built, notably North Oxford (fig. 5). The city exploded between the wars and has continued to do so since the Second World War. What was once a university town and market centre has become a regional and industrial city.

By 1200 Oxford had acquired its University, and during the fourteenth century the University gained many powers, so that the city was more or less subservient to the University until fairly recent times. There were small mediaeval suburbs north as far as St. Giles's Church, and to the east around St. Clement's Church. In 1801 Oxford had a population of just over 12,000, but by 1851, the numbers had risen to 28,000. By 1901 the population doubled again. Until 1914 Oxford grew slowly north, south, east, and west and was then primarily a university city with a large printing industry. It was still a market and sub-regional centre. The very great growth in population has been due to the development of the motor and pressed steel industries. In 1912, Morris Garages began to build motor cars at Cowley, some three miles south-east of Carfax, and the Pressed Steel Company was established at Cowley in 1926. By 1935, twenty-five per cent of all cars manufactured in the United Kingdom were made at Cowley.

The University Press (fig. 7) was established in Walton Street in 1830, and this encouraged the development of the area known as Jericho to the west of Walton Street. During the latter half of the nineteenth century, changes in the ecclesiastical nature of the colleges, and the end of the ban on married Fellows, encouraged the building of large villas for Fellows and their families along the Banbury and Woodstock Roads. Since the Second World War the undergraduate population has doubled, while the number of graduates has greatly increased. In recent years the establishment of a Polytechnic and an expanded College of Further Education have greatly increased the growth of student populations. The establishment of an expanding Regional Hospital Board and the expansion of the teaching hospitals spell further pressures and growth in the future. The language schools supply another source of students and the College of Further Education has several thousand students.

Oxford is fortunate in having large areas of open parkland within its boundaries. This open space embraces the University Parks, 'Mesopo-

Fig. 6: The High Street, from St. Mary's tower, looking east towards Magdalen and Headington Hill: note the towers and the gabled roof of the new St. Edmund Hall building on the left.

Fig. 7: The University Press building, designed by Daniel Robertson and erected in 1826-30.

tamia' of the Cherwell valley, the Botanic Gardens, and the Christ Church Meadows, in one more or less continuous belt. There are other large areas of open space at the base of Headington Hill (fig. 8), the meadowlands to the west of the city, and the flood plain between the Hinkseys and the river Thames.

The qualities of buildings in Oxford stem largely from the colour and nature of the materials. The limestones of the area, notably Taynton and Stonesfield, provided the warm honey-coloured stones for walls and roofs. Unfortunately, Headington freestone was worked from the seventeenth century, and this soft, porous, and easily eroded material has necessitated many Oxford buildings being refaced. There are several domestic buildings in the centre of Oxford that are of timber-framed construction, and indeed this method of building was common until the eighteenth century. The rich red bricks of North Oxford, old St. Ebbe's, Jericho, St. Clement's, and other parts of Oxford came to Oxford later. Bricks were manufactured at Bicester, Wheatley, Great Milton, Shiplake, Goring, Culham, and Sandford, while silver-grey bricks were also produced within the county. The coming of the railways, and before them, the canals and the river, made imported bricks a cheap substitute for the natural stone. While the centres of old villages like Iffley, the Hinkseys, Wytham, Marston, Headington, and Cowley were all of stone, the residential areas of St. Ebbe's, Grand Pont, North Oxford and Summertown, Cowley, Headington, Jericho, Osney Town, and Botley are nearly all of red brick, with occasional grey bricks or buff brick dressings. Both St. Ebbe's and Jericho had yellow bricks or buff bricks used to enliven the red brick façades.

10

Fig. 8: Open spaces are important. This is a distant view of Oxford from Headington Hill.

I have touched upon the mediaeval city within the walls. Of the Norman castle the motte remains, with one high tower and the crypt of the church of St. George. The Saxon tower of St. Michael at the North Gate is a spectacular survival of pre-Conquest times. There are many fine Norman survivals, however, including the crypt of St. Peter-in-the-East of 1130—40. Beakheads are found at St. Ebbe's Church, while outside the old walled city, Norman work is found in plenty at Iffley, St. Cross, St. Andrew at Headington, and St. James at Cowley. There is Norman work at the churches of St. Aldate and St. Giles, while the Cathedral displays much Norman work, dating from the re-foundation of the Augustinian monastic church of St. Frideswide in 1122. The great priory (later abbey) of Osney was also Augustinian, and was founded outside the walls in 1129, but of this practically nothing remains. There were many other religious houses in or near Oxford, including Godstow Abbey (only one small early sixteenth-century building survives), Rewley Abbey (now only remembered by a small arch and wall near the coalyards of the railway station), and the establishments of the Dominicans (or Blackfriars), Franciscans (or Greyfriars), Carmelites, Austin Friars, Trinitarians, Friars of the Sack, and the Crutched Friars. Of these houses practically nothing

11

Fig. 9: *Hawksmoor's All Souls College buildings from St. Mary's: 'the whole fabric of central Oxford is, almost without exception, a wonderful amalgam of fine buildings...'*

Above: fig. 10 The grandeur of New College

Facing page, above left: fig. 11 The grandest of all seventeenth-century architectural examples is the inner side of the gate tower of the Schools Quadrangle leading to the Bodleian Library.

Facing page, above right: fig. 12 Tom Tower at Christ Church (1681-2) by Sir Christopher Wren

Facing page, bottom: fig. 13 The Clarendon Building (1711-15) by Nicholas Hawksmoor

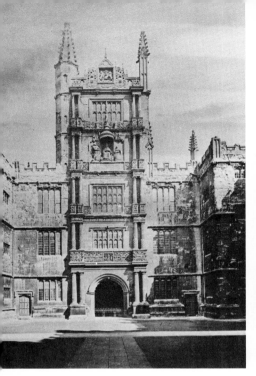

survives save the names, and not even these in most cases.

By the middle of the fifteenth century there were about seventy halls and fourteen colleges. Halls were the hostels or *hospitia* where the students lived. It is beyond the scope of this book to describe the development of the buildings of the University of Oxford. The earliest major buildings are found at Merton College. The heart of the city contains collegiate buildings dating from the thirteenth to the twentieth century. The classical formality of Queen's College is viewed with hardly a jolt after the cloistered calm of New College, and the whole fabric of central Oxford is, almost without exception, a wonderful amalgam of fine buildings, elegant spaces, grandeur, intimacy, superb vistas, glorious skylines, and wonderful sculptured detail (figs. 9—12). For the facts about Oxford's architecture the reader should turn to *Oxfordshire* in *The Buildings of England* series, by Jennifer Sherwood and Nikolaus Pevsner (Harmondsworth 1974), or to *Oxford* by Felix Markham (1967).

The mediaeval city of Oxford went through great changes before the Reformation with the building of Wolsey's college of Christ Church. The scale of the great Tom Quad is greater than that of any other Oxford quadrangle, indeed, it is uncomfortably so, especially since the cloisters were never completed. Oxford south of Carfax became greatly altered. The dissolution of the religious houses destroyed much of the mediaeval atmosphere. Various zealots founded new colleges, including St. John's and the Holy and Undivided Trinity (both Catholic, dating from 1555), and Jesus, Wadham, and Pembroke (1671, 1610 and 1624 respectively, all in a more or less Protestant cause). While Gothic was a style still used, Elizabethan and Jacobean motifs began to appear. Wadham displays much of the Jacobean style, with curious Gothic survivals. The grandest of all seventeenth-century architectural examples is the inner side of the gate tower of the Schools Quadrangle leading to the Bodleian Library (fig. 11). There was an enormous amount of collegiate work during the seventeenth century. Christopher Wren built the Sheldonian Theatre in 1663, and Tom Tower at Christ Church in 1681—2, an unforgettable silhouette (fig. 12). The best of late seventeenth-century architecture in Oxford is found in the Queen's College library building, in Trinity College Chapel (1691—4), and in the old Ashmolean Museum, opened 1683.

The eighteenth century saw the influence of Vanbrugh and Hawksmoor. The Clarendon Building, 1711—15 (fig. 13), and the North Quad of All Souls (fig. 14) are the work of Hawksmoor. Dean Aldrich added Peckwater Quad to Christ Church and All Saints Church to the High. Fine new buildings went up at Worcester and Magdalen Colleges, and in the Garden Quad of New College. The gigantic library at Christ Church, by George Clarke, begun in 1717, is grandly Roman in manner (fig. 15). Many fine ranges of collegiate buildings were erected at this time, as were many individual houses. The grandest of all Oxford's eighteenth-century buildings, the Radcliffe Camera, by James Gibbs, was built 1737—49, and is perhaps the finest domed building in England (fig. 16). Henry Keene's Radcliffe Observatory of 1772, redesigned by James Wyatt in the late 1770s, is an Adamesque interpreta-

Fig. 15: The grandly Roman library by George Clarke (begun in 1717), at Christ Church (left), dominates Peckwater.

tion of Greek Revival, an Oxonian Tower of the Winds (fig. 17).

Much refacing was carried out in the early years of the nineteenth century. The Greek Revival only really appeared at St. Paul's Church and at the Botanic Gardens, both by Underwood, although Cockerell's Ashmolean Museum (formerly the University Galleries[1]) and Taylorian Institution of 1841 both have Grecian motifs used with assurance (fig. 18). 1841 also saw the Martyrs' Memorial, a Gothic Revival Cross, by Scott.

The Ecclesiologists, the Cambridge Camden Society, the Oxford Architectural and Historical Society, and other groups gave new impetus to the Gothic Revival. Butterfield built Balliol Chapel in 1856–7, and his *tour de force*, Keble College, in polychrome brickwork, from 1868 onwards (fig. 19). Scott's magnificent Exeter College Chapel was begun in 1854 in the French Gothic style, and as a result the architect was

Fig. 16: The Radcliffe Camera (1737-49) by James Gibbs

commissioned to design the Broad Street range (1856), the library at University College (1861), and the Holywell range at New College (1872). The first large-scale High Victorian Gothic building was, however, the University Museum of 1855—60 by Deane and Woodward of Dublin (fig. 20). This building has one of the finest iron and glass interiors of the period, by Skidmore of Coventry, who also made the screen in Exeter College Chapel. The Union, of 1857, by Woodward, is also a fine Gothic building, in brick this time (fig. 21). Deane added the enormous Meadow buildings to Christ Church in 1862—6. Alfred Waterhouse added to Balliol College the Broad Street range in 1868. Street's Church of St. Philip and St. James (1860—6) is a fine building in the French Gothic style of the thirteenth century. Arthur Blomfield's Italian Romanesque Church of St. Barnabas of 1869 in Jericho is unusual in the Oxford of mid-Victorian times.

North Oxford boasts a great number of Gothic villas. Set in their own grounds, they speak eloquently of the Victorian age (fig. 22). Less eloquent, and very much out of scale, are the huge buildings of the Examination Schools (fig. 23) of 1876 and other works by Sir Thomas Jackson. However, Jackson understood how to emphasise the verticality of façades, and his work at Brasenose undoubtedly influenced Henry

Fig. 17: The Radcliffe Observatory (1772) by Henry Keene

Fig. 18: The Ashmolean, with the Taylorian beyond

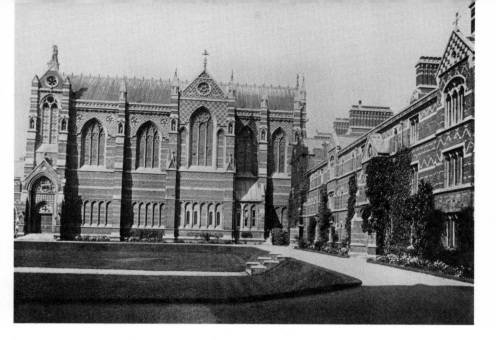

Fig. 19: Keble College, of 1868 onwards, a tour-de-force *in polychrome brickwork, by William Butterfield*

Fig. 20: The University Museum (1855-60) by Deane and Woodward

Above left: fig. 21 The Oxford Union (1857) by Woodward
Above right: fig. 22 A fine Victorian Gothic villa on the Banbury Road
Below: fig. 23 The Examination Schools (1876) by Sir Thomas Jackson

Fig. 24: The Old Town Hall . . .

Fig. 25: . . . replaced by Henry Hare's Town Hall of 1893.

Hare, whose Midland Bank and Town Hall demonstrate how large masses can be tamed by modelling.

The huge Science Area of Oxford is, alas, an area where architectural anarchy is rampant. The great mixture of styles and buildings owes little to the precedent of previous centuries, and fails to establish a new cohesion worthy of the present century. This has been partly due to what appears to have been a lack of conviction, failure of nerve, or both. After the work of Jackson, only Basil Champneys and a few others appear to have built with anything like zest, as at Merton (1908), Oriel (1911), New College (1885 and 1896), Mansfield (1887—9), St. Peter-le-Bailey (1874), and the Shelley Memorial at University College (1893). Henry Hare's Town Hall of 1893, replacing an earlier building (fig. 24), is a splendid composition riotously exuberant in its detail and assured in touch (fig. 25), as is his Midland Bank at Carfax. Stephen Salter's Lloyd's Bank is also an adventurous essay in street architecture (fig. 26).

After such late-Victorian and Edwardian excess, taste turned to chaste, even dull, essays in William and Mary, and Queen Anne. After J. J. Stevenson had built in Banbury Road (fig. 27), and Basil Champneys had started work at Lady Margaret Hall, Blomfield brought Hampton Court pomp to Oxford at Wordsworth, the first large build-

Fig. 26: Henry Hare's Midland Bank at Carfax may be seen to the left, and Lloyd's Bank, by Stephen Salter, may be seen to the right.

Above left: fig. 27 An example of a North Oxford house (c. 1880) by J.J. Stevenson
Above right: fig. 28 Ruskin College of 1912-13
Below: fig. 29 Rhodes House (1929) by Sir Herbert Baker

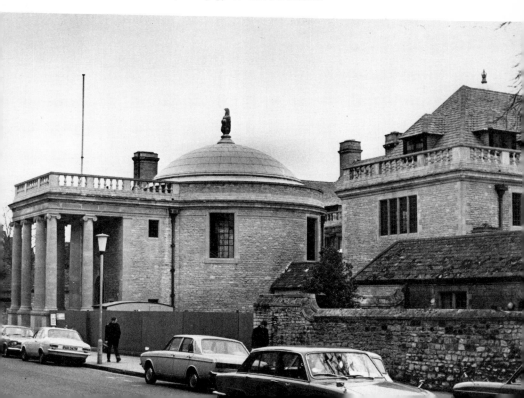

Above left: fig. 30 The New Bodleian (1937-40) by Sir Giles Scott
Above right: fig. 31 Campion Hall (1933-6) by Sir Edwin Lutyens

ing of Lady Margaret Hall. A heavy sub-William and Mary style also appears at Ruskin College (1912–13) (fig. 28), in the Organic Chemistry Building of 1913–16 by Waterhouse, and in the Pathology Building of 1926 by E. P. Warren. How dull they seem when compared with the polychrome brickwork of Butterfield's gorgeous Keble College of 1869, or with the pioneer building at the Museum of 1855–6! The present century, already in its last quarter, has not contributed a great deal of architectural splendour. Neo-Georgian, of puddingy consistency, was favoured by those who openly sneered at Keble (believing it to have been designed by Ruskin). Until Sir Albert Richardson's work at St. Hilda's of 1960–1, and that of Raymond Erith at Lady Margaret Hall in 1957–61, neo-Georgian was being erected to co-exist with a singularly unconvinced and unconvincing style derived from the work of Sir Herbert Baker, starting with Rhodes House of 1929 (fig. 29). The post-Baker manner, nearly always of honey-coloured stone, uses quite a lot of squared rubble, rather than ashlar, and owes nothing to Oxford tradition. As a cliché, it reached its apogee in Sir Giles Gilbert Scott's mammoth New Bodleian (fig. 30) of 1937–40 (an erection that replaced a fair number of pretty little historic buildings, all with vertical emphasis and domestic scale). Scott's St. Anne's of 1938–51 and Sir Hubert Worthington's Radcliffe Science Library (1933–4) continue in the post-Baker style. Lanchester and Lodge followed Worthington with a series of buildings in 1946, 1948, and 1949, all curiously unrelated, unconvincing, and lacking in style.

Two buildings stand out as being outside the Baker–Scott–Worthington reference: Campion Hall of 1933–6 by Lutyens (fig. 31), a masterpiece of assured and reticent design, and Nuffield College of

26

1939—60 (fig. 32) by Harrison, Barnes, and Hubbard (a curious attempt to marry traditional Cotswold architectural forms with collegiate buildings, but with a spire cleverly unrelated to the book-stack tower).

'Modern' architecture, in the sense of a post-war untraditional style, came to Oxford first in the industrial and housing estates, but the tight budgets and minimal standards have created unattractive areas. Possibly the first really distinguished essay in a modern un-historical architecture was the small set of rooms at Brasenose College designed by Powell and Moya in 1959—61. This is a masterpiece of reticence and good detailing, and more successful, perhaps, than their later efforts for Corpus Christi and for Christ Church, though both have their good points. The same architects have designed Wolfson College. The Architects' Co-Partnership added a modest approach to Corpus Christi College in 1957, and an agreeable range of polygons at St. John's in 1958 (fig. 33).

Fig. 32: Nuffield College (1939-60) by Harrison, Barnes and Hubbard

Perhaps the most spectacular modern building in Oxford is St. Catherine's College, designed by Arne Jacobsen with Knud Holscher as site architect (figs. 34, 35). Danish craftsmanship, elegance of detailing, and almost obsessional formality have created a clear and almost unbearably perfect set of buildings, axially planned, but unrelated to their surroundings. Near 'St. Cat.'s' is the new Law Library by Sir Leslie Martin and Colin St. John Wilson, a massive brick pile with horizontal bands of windows, and mighty steps reminiscent of an ancient temple (fig. 36). Again, though, this is very much a statement in space, and bears little relation to its surroundings.

Less successful, perhaps, are Brett and Pollen's new buildings for Exeter at the corner of Broad and Turl Streets, for the ashlar cladding ignores the traditional detailing that would have ensured freedom from the ugly weather staining this building has suffered (see chap. 2, fig. 20), whilst presenting an unnecessarily hard corner to the street. The juxtaposition of the new building to George Gilbert Scott's wonderful College Chapel seems to lack subtlety and feeling (fig. 37). Sir Hugh Casson's New Buildings at Worcester are elegant and assured for their time, but have been perhaps somewhat spoiled by recent adjacent buildings that try to be reticent, but appear to be merely weak (fig. 38). The Goodhart Quadrangle buildings at University College of 1960—61 by Robert Matthew & Johnson-Marshall are not perhaps as full of repose as they ought to be, possibly because the fenestration cannot

Facing page: fig. 33 The 1958
range of St. John's polygons,
designed by the Architects'
Co-Partnership

Right and below: figs. 34, 35,
St. Catherine's College, by Arne
Jacobsen

decide to be still, and is ever changing in emphasis. The 'Festival of Britain' roofline does not help, either.

David Roberts' Sacher Building (1961—2) for New College is, in townscape terms, unfortunate, for it is aggressively *horizontal* in emphasis whereas the rest of the street on the west side is composed of little *vertical* buildings. It is said that the architect was trying to match that wall on the opposite side of the street, but that is not the essence of Longwall Street. The same architect has been infinitely more successful at St. Hugh's, a splendid bold building in hard red brick, used with almost Butterfieldian panache, but without Butterfield's feeling for polychrome effect and detail. Here, Roberts has made a positive, grand addition to North Oxford.

Howell, Killick, Partridge and Amis have done a splendid job at St. Antony's College with their new buildings of 1971—2 (fig. 39). Their earlier buildings for St. Anne's are also interesting (fig. 40). Other

Below: fig. 36 The Law Library by Sir Leslie Martin and Colin St. John Wilson

Above: fig. 37 The junction between George Gilbert Scott's College Chapel and the new Exeter building

Fig. 38: *The new buildings at Worcester. Those on the right were designed by Sir Hugh Casson.*

Fig. 39: *St. Antony's College new buildings (1971-2) by Howell, Killick, Partridge, and Amis*

Fig. 40: St. Anne's new buildings by Howell, Killick, Partridge and Amis.
Fig. 41: The new buildings at St. John's by Philip Dowson of Arup Associates.

Fig. 42: The Nuclear Physics Building (1967)

new buildings have added to the Oxford townscape, notably by The Oxford Architects' Partnership at Balliol; by John Fryman at various sites; and, most recently, by Philip Dowson of Arup Associates at St. John's (fig. 41), following his earlier work at Somerville. Unfortunately, this architect's Nuclear Physics Building of 1967 and thereafter, built between Banbury and Keble Roads, now completely dwarfs the beginnings of North Oxford, and, by being unrelated to the existing fabric, represents a major dent in a vulnerable area. Together with the adjoining Department of Engineering buildings, by Ramsey, Murray, White and Ward, these high buildings tower over the Parks and the Banbury Road (figs. 42, 43). Much more successful, considering its bulk, is the Zoology and Psychology Building of 1965—70 from Sir Leslie Martin's office. This massive and monumental composition is handled with skill, formality, and elegance (fig. 44). Elegant the constructions of the Nuclear Physics and Department of Engineering blocks certainly are not, and, in townscape terms is far too dominating when viewed from either the street or the Parks. Perhaps the most inelegant addition to the Science Area skyline has been the Biochemistry Building of 1961—3

Fig. 43: The combination of the Engineering and Nuclear Physics blocks dominate the Banbury Road.

by Ramsey, Murray, White, and Ward, an eight-storey block of singular prosaicness (fig. 45).

The new buildings at Keble by Ahrends, Burton, and Koralek are successful designs, but perhaps are less assured in terms of the brick, a wishy-washy light brown much favoured by the City's Planning Committee and officers (fig. 46). The contrast with Butterfield's rich polychrome is almost painful. James Stirling's Florey Building for Queen's in St. Clement's is as aggressive a modern building as may be found,

Fig. 44: The Zoology and Psychology building (1965-70) by Sir Leslie Martin.

with its bright red bricks and large areas of glass, again, curiously unrelated to its surroundings, but an undeniably interesting building in itself (see chap. 6, fig. 6). The ingenious new buildings at St. Edmund Hall, by Kenneth Stevens & Associates, the executive architect being Gilbert Howes, contribute much at lower levels (fig. 47), and have added a row of gables reminiscent of the seventeenth century to the roofscape. Less happy, however, are the flues and towers, and the structure (erected 1968—70) caused heated controversy in respect of its impact on the unique skyline of Oxford (chapter 1, fig. 6).

Other interesting modern buildings include the new commercial block for Blackwell's at Hythe Bridge Street by the Oxford Architects' Partnership, an elegantly detailed work (fig. 48); the Oxford Mail and Times building by Arup Associates in Osney Mead (fig. 49), and the new buildings for Trinity and Blackwell's by Robert Maguire and Keith Murray (fig. 50). Wadham has also carried out a combined exercise

Fig. 45: The impact of the Biochemistry Building when seen from St. Mary's

Fig. 46: The new buildings at Keble by Ahrends, Burton and Koralek

with Blackwell's at the Holywell end of Wadham, to provide reticent and elegant buildings designed by Gillespie, Kidd, and Coia of Glasgow.

But most of these are quality buildings. The lessons of Oxford streetscape have been missed time and time again, as at Lord Holford's Woolworth's, where the vertical rhythms of the streets are lost in a massive horizontal sweep.

Growing population has created new areas for housing, much less agreeable than old North Oxford. Indeed, the demands for housing have contributed to the erosion of an incomparable Gothic suburb, for

Fig. 47: The new buildings at St. Edmund Hall by Gilbert Howes of Kenneth Stevens & Associates

Fig. 48: *The new Blackwell building at Hythe Bridge Street by the Oxford Architects' Partnership.*

Fig. 49: *The Oxford Mail & Times building by Arup Associates in Osney Mead.*

Right: fig. 50 The new buildings for Trinity by Robert Maguire and Keith Murray.

Below: fig. 51 Oxford's skyline is a national treasure

the large houses are largely in multiple occupation while the grounds are under pressure for development. Huge housing estates surround Oxford. Sprawl has replaced tightly-knit urban fabric.

Oxford's skyline is a national treasure. Seen from various points on the surrounding hills, the views of the centre of the city are unforgettable (fig. 51). Unfortunately, new pylons, suburban sprawl, ill-placed massive new buildings in and around Oxford, and lumpish new buildings near the heart of the old city, have all contributed to distract the eye from the historic skyline. The worst offenders are undoubtedly the University's Nuclear Physics Building and Biochemistry Block, while the new garage block at Botley, the new hospital blocks at Osler Road, and the various tower blocks of flats dotted around the city have been unhelpful.

Pleas for the conservation of Oxford are not new. On 14 November 1883 William Morris gave a lecture, in which he said:

> Go through Oxford streets and ponder on what is left us there unscathed by the fury of the thriving shop and the progressive college . . . Not only are London and other great commercial cities mere masses of sordidness, filth, and squalor, embroidered with patches of pompous and vulgar hideousness, no less revolting to the eye and the mind when one knows what it means: not only have whole counties of England, and the heavens that hang over them, disappeared beneath a crust of unutterable grime, but the disease, which, to a visitor coming from the Times of art, reason and order, would seem to be a love of dirt and ugliness for its own sake, spreads all over the country, and every little market town seizes the opportunity to imitate, as far as it can, the majesty of the hell of London and Manchester. Need I speak to you of the wretched suburbs that sprawl round our fairest and most ancient cities? Must I speak to you of the degradation that has so speedily befallen this city, still the most beautiful of

them all, a city which, with its surroundings, would, if we had a grain of common-sense, have been treated like a most precious jewel, whose beauty was to be preserved at any cost? I say at any cost, for it was a possession which did not belong to us, but which we were trustees of for all posterity . . .

. . . When I remember the contrast between the Oxford of to-day and the Oxford which I first saw thirty years ago, I wonder I can face the misery (there is no other word for it) of visiting it, even to have the honour of addressing you to-night . . . in short, our civilization is passing like a blight, daily growing heavier and more poisonous, over the whole face of the country . . . So it comes to this, that not only are the minds of great artists narrowed and their sympathies frozen by their isolation, not only has co-operative art come to a standstill, but the very food on which both the greater and the lesser art subsists is being destroyed: the well of art is poisoned at its spring.

It is a source of sober speculation to imagine what Morris would say if he were confronted by the Oxford of today. 'Scraping', re-hashing old façades to conform to a current taste, and an urge to change buildings so that current fads can be satisfied were diseases of Morris's day, as they are diseases of our own.

In 1853, Edward Burne-Jones described Oxford:

On all sides, except where it touched the railway, the city ended abruptly, as if a wall had been thrown about it, and you came suddenly upon the meadows (fig. 52). There was little brick in the city, it was either grey with stone or yellow with the wash of the pebble-dash in the poorer streets. It was an endless delight to us to wander about the streets, where were still many old houses with wood-carving and a little sculpture here and there. The Chapel of Merton College had

Fig. 52: Oxford from the Meadows

been lately renovated by Butterfield, and Pollen, a former Fellow of Merton, had painted the roof of it. Many an afternoon we spent in that chapel. Indeed I think the buildings of Merton and the Cloisters of New College were our chief shrines in Oxford.[2]

The hopes of the middle years of the nineteenth century were soon to fade in a veritable orgy of rebuilding, 'restoration', expansion, and refurbishing. The urge to get on with development at the expense of an historic past was a strong one hundred years ago. For a century the fury of the pace of change has continued, to reach a climax in the last half-century. Huge new areas have been built, and huge old areas have been razed. Villages around Oxford have become dormitory suburbs, and the motor-car, that monster that has been partially responsible for the explosion of Oxford, has also been contributing in no small part to its erosion.

[1] The Ashmolean Museum was in Broad Street in 1841. The University Galleries, by Cockerell became the Ashmolean in 1898.
[2] Quoted in *Memorials* by Georgiana Burne-Jones. (London, 1904, 1, 75)

2
Broad Street and the City Centre

'I am the Dean of Christ Church, Sir:
There's my wife; look well at her.
She's the Broad and I'm the High;
We are the University.'

C. A. Spring-Rice:
The Masque of Balliol

*Left: fig. 1 Magdalen tower from
the Botanic Gardens*

Fig. 2: The Victorians gave Christ Church Meadows their planting. Unfortunately the elms are diseased, and are being (1976) cut down.

Jacob Burckhardt and Oswald Spengler considered both the State and Cities as works of art. Differences were observed between 'culture-cities' and 'civilization-cities', the former having vigour and a sympathy with the 'cosmic beat', while the latter are old and tired and no longer become part of that indefinable metaphysical rhythm which gives significance to works of art.

Central Oxford bears all the hallmarks of a *culture-city*, and if we stand in the Botanic Gardens and look over towards Magdalen, we can see something more than just a tower: we see a work of art, a supreme achievement, no less, of European culture in these islands (fig. 1).

The Victorians, too, added to Oxford in a way which gave much to the *inscape,* or fundamental character, of the town, although it lost its compact mediaeval shape and gained a great deal which could have been done better. Our own age (which is a civilization-age, and therefore the dying phase of a true culture) has not given Oxford much that appeals to a developed aesthetic sensibility. Christ Church Meadow was really rather dreary in the eighteenth century, but the Victorians gave it the distinctive landscape of trees and avenues, river walks and charm (fig. 2). Enclosure is experienced in Christ Church Meadow, where the unique skyline of Oxford helps to give a sense of sheltered security to the open land. Fig. 3 shows the walls of Merton bounding the open space. Trees can help to give form and enclosure to what would other-

Fig. 3: Views in the open meadows to the south of Christ Church and Merton

wise be featureless landscape, and fig. 2 demonstrates how an avenue of
mature trees creates an archlike effect rather like an arcade or an airy
cathedral, and gives direction, form and structure to a view. Thickly
planted trees can give the opaqueness of a screen or very informal
buildings, so that when they enclose an open stretch of greensward,
an architectural effect is created, with only the mysterious glimpse of a
tower over the tops of the trees, and the formal structures of fine
buildings as foci. The Victorian additions to Christ Church facing the
Meadow have a period excellence as they have mellowed and gathered
a patina of creeper and warm old colours (fig. 4).

Central Oxford is not Carfax. It is the area around Radcliffe
Square (figs. 5, 6). Some have said that if all European architecture were
to be destroyed, it would be possible to reconstruct the vanished culture
from this part of Oxford. Think of the Radcliffe Camera by James
Gibbs (fig. 5); of the Divinity Schools; of Hawksmoor's All Souls
(fig. 6); of St. Mary's tremendous spire, and see how these elements set
each other off and constantly change in mood and composition as you
walk about.

Observe the textures underfoot (figs. 6—8), with the cobbles, flags,
kerbs, and details. The sense of mystery as you walk into a courtyard
towards the Bodleian is yet filled with delight and expectancy (fig. 7),
while there are few jarring notes.

Fig. 4: The formal avenue leading to the Victorian wing of Christ Church

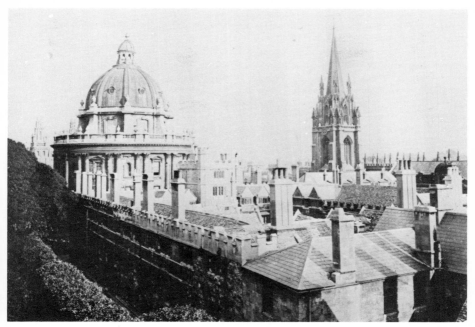

Above: fig. 5 The dome of the Radcliffe Camera showing the spire of St. Mary's.

Below left: fig. 6 The screen and chapel of All Souls, with the Camera on the right. Note the broken skyline, the intimate and subtle enclosure, and the paving.

Below right: fig. 7 A sunlit courtyard off Radcliffe Square showing the well-worn paving.

Yet all these buildings, which have in themselves metaphysical qualities, form a totality which is itself a work of art. The materials are natural stone and good lead.

Turn to any new building, let us say Cowley Centre, and what do we see? Materials which will never weather with dignity; which have no roots in the earth; and forms which by no stretch of an over-stretched imagination could have any relationship with works of art. Cowley Centre, in short, is the product of a civilization-city at the end of its life (see chap. 8).

Equally, we can turn to the Victorians and see products of their age: the churches of St. Philip and St. James (see chap. 6, fig. 15), and the Italianate St. Barnabas (see chap. 7, fig. 1). Ecclesiastically, they are marvellous buildings; as works of art they are very fine; as dominants in the townscape they could hardly be bettered.

Compare these buildings with some of the disasters discussed in other chapters, and the difference between the Spenglerian and Burck-hardtian definitions will be obvious. The all mod. con. suburbs may obey the measurable criteria laid down to ensure a free flow of high speed traffic; the requisite amounts of light in houses; suitable hygienic bathrooms; and minimal space standards. As such, they are products of a 'civilisation-city', lacking in those unmeasurable aspects that make them works of art.

The physical structures of our cities reflect our own level of culture. There are many examples of recent developments in Oxford that show the level in its true colours: a tasteless, commercially orientated society with no roots in the earth nor with any metaphysical experience in the present.

Other ages, the ages that produced a Magdalen, a Merton (fig. 9), a Radcliffe Camera, an Oxford, were of their own time, and were full of

Fig. 8: Looking south past the Camera towards St. Mary's Church. Note the textures of the paving.

Fig. 9: Merton, from the Meadows

the confidence that comes from a period or periods sure of their own
values, and with a sufficient spiritual bank-balance to be able to create
works of art.

The buildings that make up the historic core of Oxford are works
of art because they are in possession of that inner repose having its being
in that moment of purpose which created them.

The guiding principle of today is based upon that spiritual bankruptcy which is born of expediency. Its influence is everywhere to be
seen, eating away the legacies of finer ages like a cancer, out of envy, or
ignorance, or just for shame.

The Erosion of Oxford is no accident. It is a disease of the times
and is happening because the structures of our civilisation and culture
are being challenged, if not destroyed. Only an inner will to change can
stop the erosion, for the mood of the times is dangerous not only to
institutions but to their physical expressions as well.

One of the purposes of this book is to attempt to stir chords in
those who care for the environment and who are worried about what
is happening in Oxford, and elsewhere.

I am attempting to draw attention to those physical aspects which
everyone can see, and to demonstrate that the dreary suburbs illustrated
in other chapters are symbolic not only of a spiritual exhaustion, but of
the apparent lack of either a social or aesthetic conscience in the bodies
responsible. Caring about Oxford's ancient heritage, and caring about its
people, I am concerned about the failure to protect that heritage in the

Fig. 10: Cornmarket, at the turn of the century

Fig. 11: The same view today. Note the erosion

Fig. 12: Christ Church Cathedral, from the Meadows

ace of a twentieth-century philistinism.

Cornmarket, partially ruined by the hamfisted attempts since the war to convert it into High-Street-Anywhere, is so ugly now that it is questionable if serious aesthetic protest ever existed to denounce this major Erosion of Oxford (figs. 10, 11).

It is a contrast with Cornmarket to turn to the Meadow and walk here, at any time of the year, and look over to the Romanesque Cathedral (Victorianised) and see something that still entirely pleases fig. 12).

It is a source of enormous pleasure to escape from the noisy streets of Oxford that have been fouled by the exhausts of thousands of internal combustion engines, into the peace of an old garden. To walk beneath fine, mature trees, in all seasons, and to contemplate the gentle landscapes where once there was danger, war, and strife, is an ennobling experience.

Left, top: fig. 13 New College, from the gardens

Left, below: fig. 14 The city wall

Right: fig. 15 A charming domestic enclave between Holywell and New College Lane. Note especially the paving and the sense of enclosure.

Among favourite gardens may be numbered those of New College with its splendidly preserved part of the old Town Wall. New College has preserved the heritage of Oxford much better than the municipality has done in the case of the fragment of wall left in St. Ebbe's: indeed, the record of the City in this respect has been lamentable, and the obliteration not only of the wall, but of the ancient town plan must be regarded as one of the more unfortunate aspects of recent history. Within these gardens are other delights: the view of the sturdy Church of St. Peter-in-the-East and the grand yet friendly pile of the College itself (fig. 13). Some idea of the scale and grandeur of Oxford's Wall may be gained by walking round the remaining parts (fig. 14). Near by, the exquisite textures, almost sensual in their appeal, found in narrow alleys between domestic buildings in the vernacular tradition, speak eloquently of craftsmanship, love of materials, and an understanding of scale (fig. 15). In Queen's Lane, the glorious library of Queen's College brings an Olympian scale to what otherwise is a narrow, walled, mediaeval setting (fig. 16). This is an admirable example of how another age added its own contribution to the urban fabric, *enhancing* the character, rather than eroding it. This was before the days of Conservation Areas and long before complicated bureaucratic machinery was set up to ensure good 'planning'.

Fig. 16: Queen's College Library, from the Lane

Let us examine the Broad. In late-Victorian times it had recently acquired Waterhouse's new Balliol buildings. There were few items of street furniture to detract from the buildings, and the impact of traffic was minimal. There were pavements, but the carriageway was simply gravel. The domestic buildings on the right of the picture, part of Trinity College, should be noted, for it was in connection with these that William Morris took up the cudgels on behalf of unpretentious buildings (fig. 17). He might well have been making a plea for the Charles Street houses in St. Ebbe's, for the old houses in Castle Street or for the fine old buildings that once stood at the corner of the Broad and Parks Road. Gloucester Green had its quota of ancient houses, while even George Street was graced by many potentially conservable ancient buildings, not one of which remains. Morris wrote to the *Daily News* on 20 November 1885. His words are as true ninety years later as the day he penned them. The losses since then have been catastrophic, despite his admirable arguments. This is what he wrote:

I wish to ask if it is too late to appeal to the mercy of the 'Dons' to spare the few specimens of ancient town architecture which they have not yet had time to destroy, such, for example, as the little plaster houses in front of Trinity College or the beautiful houses left on the north side of Holywell Street. *These are in their way as important as the more majestic buildings to which all the world makes pilgrimage.*[1] Oxford thirty years ago, when I first knew it, was full of these treasures; but Oxford 'culture', cynically contemptuous of the knowledge which it does not know, and steeped to the lips in the commercialism of the day, has made a clean sweep of most of them; but those that are left are of infinite value, and still give some character above that of Victoria Street or Bayswater to modern Oxford. Is it impossible, Sir, to make the authorities of Oxford, town and gown, see this, and stop the destruction?

Fig. 17: Broad Street in Victorian times, with Waterhouse's new Balliol buildings dominating. Note the domestic buildings on the right.

Fig. 18: Broad Street in recent times. Note the harsh new Exeter building on the left at the corner of Turl Street; the traffic, the clutter; and the trees at the end of the street in the churchyard of St. Mary Magdalene.

Left: fig. 19 The Martyrs' Memorial in St. Giles'

Right: fig. 20 Broad Street, from the west, with the Clarendon Building at the end, and the cupola of the Sheldonian. Note the harshness of the new Exeter building at the corner of the Turl.

If Morris could only see the mess that has been made of St. Aldate's (practically wholly gone on one side, and partially on the other); the destruction of Castle Street; the erosion of Cornmarket; the ruination of the High at its extremities; the rebuilding of George Street; the new buildings in Longwall; and the overall loss of national treasures, we can be sure that a howl of agonised rage would soon put the fear of God into the despoilers.

The Broad today still has the little buildings by Trinity, but almost totally reconstructed in the 1960s. A hard new block at the corner of the Turl has not improved matters, but the visual clutter and sea of cars are the greatest changes (fig. 18). The odd thing about the Broad is its curious lack of focus. It is in some ways a street lacking a focal point, or centrepiece. It runs along the line of the old Town Ditch and it was in its centre that the martyrs Cranmer, Latimer, and Ridley were burnt at the stake in times when theological dogma aroused similar passions

Left: fig. 21 *The 'mock-up' of the Carfax Conduit standing outside Exeter College.*

Right: fig. 22 *A curiosity*

to those found today among adherents to even more tedious isms formulated by nineteenth- and twentieth-century gurus. The spot of the conflagration is marked by a cross set in the tarmac, and Scott's Victorian memorial to the martyrs stands round the corner, in St. Giles', adjacent to the churchyard of St. Mary Magdalene (fig. 19). The Broad is 'stopped' at its eastern end by the Clarendon building's classic scale, and the cupola of the Sheldonian appears over the roofs. The hard, foursquare block of the new Exeter building at the corner of the Turl ignores principles of modelling, weathering, and the essential *vertical* elements that compose the street (fig. 20). The placing of the restored Scott memorial on the site of the martyrdom would give a much-needed emphasis to the empty heart. Perhaps a site to the west of the junction of the Turl and the Broad would be best, not obscuring the view of Trinity Gates and Chapel. An alternative monument for this site that I suggested years ago was the old Carfax Conduit, now at Nuneham Courtenay (fig. 21).

Touches of humour enliven the Oxonian scene from time to time. A bicycle, suspended from a lamp-post, perhaps (fig. 22), or some classic of graffiti, such as:

'Matriculation makes you blind'

or, even better,

'God is Dead. (signed) Nietzsche'

beneath which, in another hand,

'Nietzsche is Dead. (signed) God'

cause ripples of amusement. They are essentially ephemeral, however, and diverting though they are, it is the more permanent aspects of the physical fabric of Oxford with which I am concerned.

It is but a step to Magpie Lane, where, as one looks back, the astonishing profusion of riches that is St. Mary's spire terminates the vista. It is quite remarkable how this beautiful and distinctive spire dominates so many alleyways and streets, and must be seen as no accident, but as a consciously conceived aesthetic principle of the mediaeval builders (fig. 23).

To the south, down Magpie Lane, another pleasing enclosure of street and terminal vista is found composed of stones, timber, stucco, and small elements such as the lamp (fig. 24) that guides the eye to the tower of Merton College. The same principle of framing and enclosure is found in Radcliffe Square as it is entered from the High. The textures underfoot relate to the architecture, and are most important in the over-all scheme.

It is again apparent how strategically placed trees can play an important part in the townscape, for, although the tree in the High is justly famous (see chap. 3, fig. 39), it is less well-known that the same principle is applied to many other streets in Oxford. Kybald Street (fig. 25) is still pleasing, and it is particularly pleasant to record a traditional lamp on a new building. The tree is especially fine, and the lovely little house at the end is framed by the College and by Kybald Twychen. Magpie Lane is no exception. Looking north, we discover a magnificent tree that hangs over Oriel wall, and that adds to the qualities of an already wonderful space where all the elements combine in a pleasing whole (fig. 26). This tree in summer is magnificent. When we look north towards Oriel, the new Corpus building seems to be successful.

It is somewhat disappointing, therefore, to look south down Magpie Lane today towards Merton tower and to see the new Corpus building from this viewpoint. A strange note of unease is struck by the disruption of the streetscape. A restlessness is sensed about the roofline, and something odd happens in terms of proportion. The bollards do not help, those architectural gimmicks so beloved in the 1960s. The old houses that used to stand on the site were similar to those on the left of fig. 27 and some idea of the scale and proportion of the old buildings may be gauged from the surviving groups in Magpie Lane. Basically, the problems of the new buildings can be summed up in the words: scale and materials. To attempt a verticality was undoubtedly right, but the projecting bays of the two elements flanking the central blank stone wall are really too wide. The materials,

Facing page: fig. 24 Magpie Lane looking south. Note the textures, the lamp, the enclosure and the scale.

Above left: fig. 25 Kybald Street, with the new Corpus building on the right

Above right: fig. 26 Magpie Lane looking north after the new Corpus building had been erected. The bollards are presumably to stop people banging their heads on the projecting bays.

Right: fig. 27 The new Corpus building in Magpie Lane with Merton in the background. The old buildings on the left are similar to those the Corpus building replaced.

Fig. 28 Longwall with the new Sacher building.

lead and white exposed-aggregate concrete, are very harsh in such a
situation. The two bays create an unhappy duality, so that the façade
is unresolved about its centre. Elsewhere in Magpie Lane we find
stucco, ashlar, and some rubble on garden walls, but generally speaking,
the buildings of Oxford, if they are of stone, are of ashlar work, with
the exception of garden walls. Admittedly, Kybald Twychen is rubble
and plaster, but the rubble on the Corpus building is not used in a traditional manner, but is built in panels, a distressingly familiar motif
seemingly previously encountered in the Woolworth's building in
Cornmarket.

Yet if we compare the Corpus building with the Sacher building
in Longwall, we see that the basic problem of creating small-scale
vertical elements was partially understood in the former case. Perhaps
the lessons of simple vertical rectangular voids in plain walls provided
by the original buildings on the site might have been learned, however,
with benefit. The *degree* of scale has clearly been misjudged, so that
we are left with a curiously unsatisfying solution to the problem. Many
have praised the Corpus building, but many have questioned the basis
of its design.

The Sacher building, on the other hand, *is* faced with ashlar. So
far, so good, but when it is examined in the context of the street, the
jolt is shocking (fig. 28). Longwall consists of a long stone battle-
mented wall on the right and used to consist of a row of pleasant three-
storeyed houses on the left, the west, side. The houses were generally
plaster-faced on timber frames, with simple windows of *vertical*

64

emphasis punched into the walls. The whole street was essentially domestic in character and consisted of numbers of houses, all *vertical* in terms of their façades. All the roofs were of a simple slate-covered form draining to gutters above the façades. The Sacher building is aggressively *horizontal* in emphasis, and pays absolutely no attention to either the scale or the character of the existing street. It is said that the designer tried to marry the new façade with the idea of the wall opposite, but even that notion does not bear examination when we look at the photograph. A flat roof, horizontal bands of windows, and horizontal strips of cill and cope, all add up to a dismissal of the qualities of old Longwall. The designers of the other new building have been much more careful (fig. 29), and have accentuated the verticality of the street, but the ground-floor storey is very drab in treatment, while some of the lessons of simple vertical voids in plain walls might have rubbed off with more agreeable and less forced results than those displayed in the fussy upper storeys. The Sacher Building has no plinth, and does not grow logically from the pavement. It brutalises the corner, and must be one of the least successful pieces of infill in old Oxford. Graffiti and other aspects of unrest have recently been appearing, and the plain wall of the ground-floor storey of the Sacher Building provides a perfect writing surface.

Little Clarendon Street, too, has changed in character with

Left: fig. 29 A new building in Longwall by the Oxford Architects' Partnership

Right: fig. 30 Little Clarendon Street. The small domestic buildings on the left were typical of this street as it used to be.

Fig. 31: The coarse bulk of the new building in Little Clarendon Street on the right. For a change, the upper storeys are less happy than the shop fronts. The aggressive horizontality ignores the small-scale vertical emphasis of the street.

rebuilding. This formerly interesting and diversified street consisted of small, vertical elements, similar to those in fig. 30 on the left (northern) side. Here small shops rubbed shoulders with a pub, and the whole was interesting. The new buildings have overwhelmed the street (fig. 31) but unusually, the ground-floor shop-fronts in Little Clarendon Street are moderately successful: it is what goes on up above that has been so unfortunate. The very coarse cantilever of the first building (fig. 30) is a disaster in townscape terms, whilst the jumble of unrelated buildings has failed to create any cohesion in this once-pleasant little street. The blank walls however, provide suitable background for the graffiti purveyors (fig. 32).

All these buildings have been through an expensive planning process. All have been designed by architects. It is quite clear that public discussion of new buildings must be stimulated. We are told what to like and what to despise by the arbiters of taste, the glossies, the pundits, and other apologists. Let us look at these buildings and others with uncloudy eyes, and exercise judgement, argue in public, debate the issues and put the various cases.

We have all heard a lot about public participation in planning. Schemes must be published in good time for discussion, and not decided behind the closed doors of an *in camera* planning committee. In the eighteenth and nineteenth centuries, architectural proposals were subjected to vitriolic attack and violent public discussion. The mystique of not arguing about architecture and our environment must be abandoned if we are to have a truly enlightened process whereby we can hammer something out in public. Squeamishness must go, and a return to honest criticism and reasoned argument must replace Pavlovian attitudinising and conditioned posturing where non-measurable aspects of our lives are involved.

Fig. 32: Graffiti in Little Clarendon Street.

3

The Central Shopping
Streets of the City

'Yet if at last, not less her lover,
You in your hansom leave the High;
Down from her towers a ray shall hover —
Touch you, a passer-by!'

Sir Arthur Quiller-Couch: *Poems.*
'Alma Mater'

*Facing page: fig. 1 The beautiful
urn in the Botanic Gardens*

Right: fig. 2 Cornmarket today. Note the impact that Littlewood's (left foreground), and Woolworth's (the large block on the left in the centre of the picture) have made.

Facing page, top: fig. 3 Cornmarket in late-Victorian times. In the centre of the picture is the Saxon tower of the Church of St. Michael-at-the-North-Gate. The 'Tea-Blenders' building on the right is actually basically a fifteenth-century structure. Note the scale of the shop fronts and the essential verticality.

Facing page, bottom: fig. 4 The same view today

The woods, parks and gardens of the city are most beautiful in May and June (fig. 1), and even as summer draws to a close, the trees of North Oxford appear as assets other less fortunate towns could well envy.

Furthermore, the centre of Oxford, now it has been cleaned thanks to a substantial grant, is looking splendid, and the colour of the stone is brought out by the sunlight. Compared with other cities and towns, central Oxford has been spared the worst excesses of cheapness and vulgarity in terms of materials. Plastics and chrome exist in Oxford, but not in such vast quantities as in other places not so far away.

Cornmarket, overcrowded and disagreeable though it is, and even with the particularly unfortunate erections by three large stores, is hardly less obnoxious when compared with other similar streets elsewhere. Erosion undoubtedly has taken place here, and the enormous problems of overcrowded streets; of destruction of scale; and of unsympathetic massing and materials are well illustrated in Cornmarket (fig. 2). Note the harshness of the elements and how destructive are the shop signs on deep fascias which create a strongly horizontal line in a street of small vertical units (apart from the three lumpish stores). Yet even in Cornmarket, stone, stucco and paint still predominate despite the glaring introduction of unsympathetic materials and the gross mis-

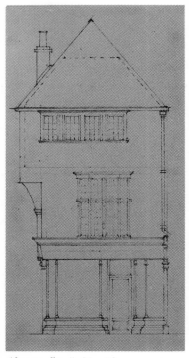

Above: fig. 5 Mr. Thomas Rayson's survey drawing of the building at the corner of Ship Street and Cornmarket before restoration.

use of stone. Oxford is an ashlar city, and rubble is foreign to it except for garden walls and a few churches.

It is worth taking a nostalgic look at Cornmarket as it was in late-Victorian times (fig. 3). The street was quiet, dominated by the two towers of St. Michael-at-the-North-Gate and St. Mary Magdalene. St. Michael's tower is a fine late-Saxon structure, approximately a thousand years old. Many of the buildings were mediaeval, usually of a timber-framed construction, but refaced at various times. The shop-fronts were small in scale and the glazing was subdivided. Lettering was hand-painted. The rhythm was essentially vertical. Fig. 4 shows the same view as it is today.

Two buildings stand out as excellent examples of restoration. The fifteenth-century building adjacent to the tower of St. Michael's was restored by the architect, Mr. Thomas Rayson between the Wars. Mr. Rayson found that the original structure was covered with nineteenth-century hand plaster that was badly cracked and thought to be unsafe. The building was mutilated with advertisements externally. The west end of the roof was finished with a hipped roof of early nineteenth-century hard plaster that was badly cracked and thought to be unsafe to end in a gable. When the main roof tie-beam of the gable was exposed,

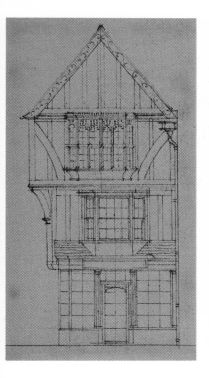
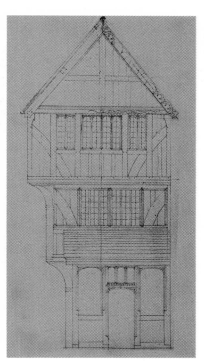

Facing page, right: fig. 6 The fifteenth-century building at the corner of Ship Street and Cornmarket in 1974. Above left: fig. 7 Mr. Thomas Rayson's preliminary scheme for the restoration. Above right: fig. 8 Mr. Thomas Rayson's second scheme for the restoration.

two horizontal mortices were found that indicated there had been a corbelled window there originally. Mr. Rayson designed a corbel window to suit the situation. The window-openings of the first floor existed, but had been partly destroyed and replaced by unworthy features all of which were removed and replaced. The ground-floor angle main post was exposed, and the shop-windows designed to leave it on show. The shop-windows themselves were designed with glazing bars of a typical eighteenth-century type essentially small in scale. The building was officially considered fit for demolition, but Mr. Rayson argued the case for restoration with notable success (figs. 5-8).

The Old Plough Inn at the corner of St. Michael Street (formerly New Inn Hall Street) is the other notable example of good restoration work. This was a simple building with an eighteenth-century front on the ground floor, a row of lead-glazed windows on the first floor, and an eighteenth-century cornice surmounted by two pediments. Behind the pediments was a large gable with a small centre window. The remainder of the building was a stone structure of an earlier date (fig. 9). Considerable demolitions were necessary, but Mr. Rayson partially preserved the front. Three pieces of moulded stone were discovered from which the architect fashioned a niche on the St. Michael's Street side of the main

Above left: fig. 9 The old Plough Inn in late-Victorian times

Above right: fig. 10 The old Plough Inn: today it is a shop

angle of the buildings to contain a figure of St. Michael. Except for the
windows of the east end of the first floor and the main roof gable, the
whole of the building is the work of Mr. Rayson. The shop windows
with glazing bars were designed in sympathy, but these have recently
been removed, thereby spoiling the scale of the shop-front (fig. 10).
This is typical erosion of detail that ruins a building of quality. The
building, however, is still right in terms of the street and the site, while
the small tobacconist's kiosk next door, though undistinguished, and
with poor lettering and unsympathetic materials, still has a *vertical*
emphasis in the street, which helps enormously.

Cornmarket happily possesses views of Tom Tower at one end
and the trees of St. Mary's Churchyard at the other. These trees are
particularly important, and it would be disastrous were they to go. Fig. 4
shows the importance of these trees at the northern end of Cornmarket.
In the churchyard itself are many old gravestones; it is to be hoped
that in the churchyards of St. Mary Magdalene and St. Giles they will
be allowed to remain as they are, and that no misguided persons will
advocate their removal or re-arrangement. They are as much a part of
the heritage of Oxford as the other memorials and buildings (fig. 11).

There are still other good things about Cornmarket. The two
marvellous banks at the Carfax end, for example, are both superb
examples of how to turn corners architecturally and successfully (see
chap. 1, fig. 29). The Saxon tower of St. Michael's Church is splendid
of its type. The view from Cornmarket along St. Michael's Street
(fig. 12) to the Methodist church spire, with a delicious Victorian
building on the left and 'Vanbrugh's House' (fig. 13) on the right

Above: fig. 11 The tombstones in the churchyard of St. Mary Magdalene. They are an important part of the heritage of Oxford.

Below left: fig. 12 St. Michael's Street, formerly New Inn Hall Street, with the spire of the Methodist Church in the distance, and the Plough Inn building on the left.

Below right: fig. 13 Vanbrugh House, St. Michael's Street

Above left: fig. 14 Ship Street

Above right: fig. 15 No. 10 Ship Street in its setting

offers its own delights. The vista along Ship Street from Cornmarket towards Scott's magnificent Exeter College Chapel is framed by a huddle of domestic buildings of decent quality and scale luckily conserved in the centre of the city (fig. 14). The old house on the corner of Ship Street and Cornmarket has already been described, but in the context of both a corner site and the proximity of St. Michael's Street, this building is very important indeed. (An over-heated hot-dog stand nearly ended this building's life some years ago.)

Both St. Michael's Street and Ship Street are significant examples of streets where the human scale is unspoiled; where enclosure is of

Fig. 16: The lettering formerly on Elliston's shop

Fig. 17: The shopfront of what used to be Elliston and Cavell's

paramount importance; and where the eye is held by an end-vista or
terminal point. It is most important to preserve these small, domestic
buildings to act as foils to the more spectacular college buildings, and
not only in Ship Street, but in Merton Street, Magpie Lane, and elsewhere. Ship Street, incidentally, boasts the oldest Council House in
Oxford, No. 10, a bijou residence originally erected for the night-
watchman centuries ago (fig. 15).

The beautiful Edwardian shop-front of what used to be Elliston
and Cavell's survives. The façade of Elliston's catches the sun on its
mellow stonework. It used to catch the light on its gilded lettering,
but unfortunately the letters have vanished from the ironwork recently
owing to the renaming of the store (fig. 16). However, the fine front
remains easy on the eyes (fig. 17). Beside this façade the well-detailed

Fig. 18: Jaeger's shopfront
Fig. 19: George Street. A case where a great deal of improvement could take place.

Left: fig. 20 A photograph of Cornmarket taken at the turn of the century showing the lost Roebuck Hotel on the right.

Right: fig. 21 The same view taken today. The massive blocks of Littlewood's on the left and Marks and Spencer's on the right, together with all the deep fascias, make a tremendous difference.

front of Messrs. Jaeger's establishment (fig. 18) brings a note of polished modern refinement, a welcome change compared with the hideous vulgarity of so much of Cornmarket, George Street, and Queen Street. The difficulty with the mess of materials, signs and glass is that the vulgarities are not even full-blooded, in a way that the stalls of the St. Giles's Fair are vulgar. Instead, they are cheap-looking, shoddy in general, and capable of a great deal of improvement (fig. 19). There are far too many jarring colours, signs and pseudo-genteel lettering. The influence of Eric Gill and the model of the Festival of Britain have tended to kill a full-blooded decorative tradition in commercial art. It would be of benefit to the traders, to Oxford, and to everyone, if these streets could be improved, simply by a fresh approach to shop-fronts and signs. It is a matter for conjecture as to why so much marble, plastic, and other inappropriate materials managed to get through an expensive planning-control machinery. It is so often the little things, as much as the elephantine mistakes, that mar our surroundings.

Cornmarket at the turn of the century was a more agreeable place than it is now. The old picture (fig. 20) shows the Roebuck Hotel on the right (another sad loss), while elsewhere in the street the steady rhythm of small, *vertical* units is evident. The same view today shows how much damage has been done. The brutal slab at the corner of Market Street catches the eye, while the deep horizontal fascias and chaotic ground-floor fronts disrupt the visual cohesion almost completely (fig. 21). Looking the other way towards Carfax, we still see the Midland Bank building and the upper storeys above Burton's (figs. 22, 3), but the ground floor of the Burton block has been ripped out, so that the block no longer appears to grow logically from the pavement. The three build-ings between the bays of Burton's and the other buildings with bays on the right have been demolished. The simple four-storey building next to

79

Top: fig. 22 Cornmarket looking towards Carfax at the turn of the century

Above right: fig. 23 The same site today

Below right: fig. 24 Brutal horizontal elements in Cornmarket. The building seems to have lost all its front teeth on the ground floor, while the upper storeys cannot decide whether they are horizontal or vertical in emphasis.

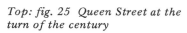

Top: fig. 25 Queen Street at the turn of the century

Above right: fig. 26 Queen Street in 1969

Below right: fig. 27 Queen Street in 1974

Fig. 28: The new entrance to Westgate

Burton's was no great loss, but the disappearance of the pretty little
Venetian structure beside it is to be regretted. The greatest tragedy,
however, was the demolition of the marvellous Gothic block with the
gables, arcaded ground floor, and balcony. All three buildings, each
vertical in emphasis, and each growing from the pavement, have been
replaced by the crude and insensitive block with the set-back ground
floor. A little further back another example of bad ground-floor
detailing may be seen (fig. 24). Here the building seems to have lost its
'front teeth' on the ground floor while the upper storeys cannot decide
whether they are horizontal or vertical in emphasis.

   Queen Street was never particularly beautiful. A photograph
taken at the turn of the century (fig. 25) shows the portion that
branches right into the New Road, and left down to what was Castle
Street. The French roofs of the Salvation Army Citadel may be seen.
The buildings on the right, in New Road, stood until the late 1960s,
and contained fine old shopfronts. Some of the lettering, however, was
insensitive in the extreme and that of Taylor's Boot Market must equal
some of the worst eyesores of today. The building on the corner (Singer
Sewing Machines), however, was replaced in the 1920s. A view along
Queen Street in early 1969 showed this building, known as 'Mac-
fisheries Corner', together with the general chaos of shoppers, traffic,
and architectural anarchy (fig. 26).

   Photographs taken in 1974 show a distinct environmental improvement. The street has been pedestrianised and paved over from wall to
wall. People can now shop in comfort and in safety (fig. 27). The

aggressively horizontal fascia of the Co-op, the group on the left (an institution the house-style of which leaves very much to be desired in terms of respecting existing street frontages throughout the country), does not help the scale of the street, however. The new Library and entrance to the Westgate Centre, whatever the shortcomings in terms of detailing, does give a focus at the end of the street, and gives a sense of enclosure. Further west, the prospect is less pleasing, and again inappropriately coloured bricks are used (the ubiquitous light brown variety so beloved by the planners) for the Library end-wall. The irritating little flower boxes seem placed for pedestrians to trip over. Planners of precincts should learn that landscaping needs to be designed as part of the scheme, and not left to the arbitrary positioning of geranium-pots.

The entrance to the Westgate Centre, a pedestrian precinct, has come out fairly well in townscape terms (fig. 28) but there remain questions of detailing and finishes that have not been too satisfactorily resolved. For instance, the quality of the concrete and brick finishes could have been better, and the thin metal sheeting of the ducting has an impermanent air.

Round the corner, in Castle Street, something of what has been lost may be gauged from the old photograph (fig. 29). The gabled timber-framed buildings on the right were fine examples of the vernacular buildings common from late-mediaeval times. The fronts were probably eighteenth-century, but the structures were very likely much earlier. The bizarre Salvation Army Citadel, complete with iron cresting on the French roofs, was an unhappy Victorian addition to the street. The interesting old buildings on the left should also be noted. Fig. 30 shows the change. On the left is part of the Westgate development, a very grisly corner, designed to the dictates of traffic, with an ugly barrier. The pedestrian underpass runs underneath this re-aligned street. Apart from the loss of many fine old buildings, many of which

Left: fig. 29 A late-Victorian view of Castle Street showing the old buildings and the Victorian Salvation Army Citadel.

Right: fig. 30 The same site in 1974

Fig. 31: Queen Street looking east at Carfax in 1974

had disappeared long before Westgate was mooted, there are serious objections to the changes. First of all, the re-alignment of Castle Street has obliterated part of the historic town plan of Oxford. Secondly, the southern part of the development is built over the line of the city wall — a line that was still clearly visible in both the Ordnance Survey and in the building alignments. Thirdly, many small businesses were forced out, although theoretically they had options to come into the new development. Nearly all new major shopping developments put minor businesses out of count because of the levels of rents and rates, while the concept of 'zoning' removed small industries and services from the hearts of areas which actually need such enterprises. Similarly, small repair workshops, or traders, cannot survive in an 'industrial estate' or 'shopping centre' because the social and economic base is denied them. Large 'planned developments', therefore, automatically favour monopolies, big combines, and the like, while the small necessary businesses that give life and service to a community are systematically destroyed.

The pedestrianisation of Queen Street, however, is a step in the right direction, as the illustrations demonstrate (figs. 29-31). If Westgate stops the eye one way, the spire of the former Church of St. Martin and All Saints acts similarly when viewed from the west. At Carfax itself, the traffic still roars through, but the townscape potential is still magnificent. Even such a large building as the Town Hall (see chap. 1, fig. 28) in St. Aldate's was handled beautifully by its designer, for the mass is broken up into a series of modelled vertical elements, with gables and a magnificent pile-up of eclectic *motifs* on the roof.

Above: fig. 32 Shops in the High showing vertical emphasis.

Right: fig. 33 Magdalen College tower, from the west

The High is generally agreeable, save for some erosion in terms of shop-fronts at the western end. Planning controls have been applied to the High, and the qualities of verticality, of human scale, of good materials, and of style, all in all, have been fairly respected (fig. 32). It was Thomas Sharp, in his *Oxford Replanned* (1948) who admirably analysed the properties of Oxford's unique High Street, the most important thoroughfare of the city, and one of Europe's greatest urban experiences. The subtleties of this gently curved street were fully understood by Dr. Sharp, and his townscape analysis remains a seminal work of the period, though his proposals, it is submitted, would have constituted a major erosion of other areas of the city. Indeed, it is perhaps fair to criticise Dr. Sharp for his view of St. Ebbe's that partly helped to create a climate of opinion to enable the destruction of a living part of the city to take place. However, Dr. Sharp's understanding of The High is beyond criticism. From the great terminal feature of Magdalen College Tower (fig. 33) to Carfax, The

Fig. 34: The High from Magdalen tower, showing the famous curved street.

High is a magnificent, coherent, and grand essay in urban design unparalleled elsewhere. The curve of the street is best appreciated from Magdalen Tower, where the eye picks out the dome of the Camera, St. Mary's Spire, All Saints', and, on the left, the towers of Merton and Christ Church (fig. 34). To the west of Magdalen, a group of buildings on the north side obeys the criterion of vertical emphasis and domestic scale (fig. 35), and, although they have undergone some reconstruction and considerable vicissitudes, remain much the same in feeling today. The subtle front of Queen's College, with its screen, is a magnificent Baroque composition, and, although symmetrical, has its centre played down so as not to dominate the street. Further west, the spire of St. Mary's comes into view, with the famous tree before it (fig. 37); its spire and pinnacles obsessively puncture the sky, in a thrusting upwards, breaking the scale down to intimate detail, and disguising the sheer bulk of the building. In the distance, another vertical form appears, in the spire of All Saints' Church. Looking back, even Queen's is vertical in its rhythms, while the buildings on the south side obey the same laws (fig. 36). Indeed, the essential verticality of Oxford is everywhere to be seen, and a view over the rooftops from the Castle area demonstrates this (fig. 38).

Fig. 35: Queen's College and the domestic scale of the buildings on the right

Fig. 36: Queen's looking east

Facing page: fig. 37 St. Mary's spire comes into view. Note the tree.

Facing page, top: fig. 38 Oxford's sky-line from the Castle area

Facing page, bottom: fig. 39 Shops in the Broad

Right: fig. 40 The exterior of the Grapes Inn, George Street, as it was.

The smaller shops in The Broad (fig. 39) are essentially human in scale, and do not sweep through several frontages to be combined in one. Therefore they obey the decencies and do not enter into that spirit of brashness that characterises the larger buildings in Cornmarket. In the same spirit is the delightful frontage of The Grapes in George Street, one of the few bright spots in this drab street (fig. 40). It is a charming façade, of terracotta with timber infill. The splendid interior, once sub-divided into snug little bars, has been considerably altered in recent years. Today it is one large space.

When we discuss *scale*, confusion tends to arise, for people do not generally know what the term means. Oxford has a scale of its own: intimate, human, intricate and agreeable. Large buildings do not necessarily have an overpowering scale, for if they have modelling which tends to break up the large areas of wall, roof, or mass, the scale is reduced and so the building becomes humane and pleasant. Take the Radcliffe Camera, for example (fig. 41): it is an enormous building, but by the intricacies of its modelling, columns, pilasters, mouldings, and the sizes of the stones of which it is built, it becomes not at all overpowering. If you can imagine a huge drum with smooth plastic surfaces and no modelling at all in the same place, you will see what a difference of scale there can be where buildings may be of the same size. Oxford is full of buildings and instances where modulation and intricacy contribute to a pleasantly human and Oxfordian scale; but there are some instances where lack of such modelling ruins the scale of streets, as in Cornmarket; and I have tried to demonstrate other examples where shops are sympathetic to the scale of the environment. One shopping area that presents its scale and qualities admirably is the Covered Market, a remarkably fine Victorian structure (fig. 42).

It must be emphasised that these points of townscape and archi-tectural detail reflect on policies of planning control. There has been insufficient care taken where Oxford's shopfronts have been concerned, and where some fronts have gone through the process of planning control, the genius of Oxford's streets has been sadly misunderstood, as has been the scale of its townscape and its building in far too many cases.

Facing page; fig. 41 The Radcliffe Camera
Below: fig. 42 The Covered Market

4

Street Lights and Other Details

'Noon strikes on England, noon on Oxford town,
Beauty she was statue cold – there's blood upon her gown.'

James Elroy Flecker:
The Dying Patriot

Above: fig. 1 The approach to Norham Gardens and Banbury Road, in 1969. The surface of the road dominates even the buildings.

Right: fig. 2 Textures in Radcliffe Square

The physical town around us is made up of many things: not just buildings and roads, but trees, walls, railings, street furniture, water, and countless little details which combine to form a whole. Of course, towns are for people, and all the activities in which people take part, but in this book it is intended to look at those subtle and unspectacular aspects of Oxford which are generally missed among the immediately significant and well-known buildings.

There has been much concern recently, and rightly, about the amount of destruction of fine buildings of all periods, but under our very eyes, and almost daily, changes are being made which are essentially ruinous to the quality of our environment.

In the late 1960s an enormous number of arrows, bollards, lines, stripes, lettering and islands appeared all over Oxford contributing to the erosion of the visual qualities of the City (fig. 1). Of course, it is argued that the bollards and islands are for the safety of pedestrians, but there are less hideous ways of doing the same thing (fig. 2). In Holland, for example, different textures of road surface and differing patterns are used to distinguish between the paths and the carriageway. Brick paviors are used on the Continent, with admirable results. The visual disasters at so many road junctions in Oxford are causes of great concern.

Another matter which should cause us alarm is the destruction of old lamps. Many of these are of pleasing design, and many were unobtrusively fixed to the walls of buildings. In recent times, the old lamps were disappearing to be replaced by the last word in sheer ugliness.

95

Not content with erecting these monstrosities to stand alone, the authorities plastered them with signs. Often, there were examples with no fewer than three signs on them (fig. 3). These new lamps were not fixed to buildings, so posts proliferated and contributed to further destruction of the amenities of streets. While it is not suggested that the older lamps are suitable for through-traffic routes, there is a very strong argument for leaving the older Victorian type of lamp-posts in the side streets, especially those of some age, to be in character with the buildings. Even if the level of lighting is not satisfactory, modern lights can be placed within the older lamp-casings.

While it now appears to be official policy to retain lamps of the traditional Windsor pattern in certain Conservation Areas, and indeed to provide new Windsor lanterns where necessary, the fight to get such a policy accepted was extremely strenuous, as well as time-consuming. The environmental lobby had to give up a very considerable amount of time to put a strong case to the local authority, which boasted an Engineer's Department, the opinions of which, apparently, were of greater import than the views of the Department of the Planning Officer, a not uncommon state of affairs in Britain. All sorts of arguments were put forward that threatened the old lamps and favoured the new. It took literally weeks of very hard work and considerable research to put up an alternative argument. The local authority official, therefore, backed by a Council and the never-empty pockets of the ratepayers, has almost limitless powers. The concerned public, however, has to go to considerable expense to persuade its own elected members *and own officials* not to destroy amenity.

Facing page, far left: fig. 3 An ugly modern lamp with three signs fixed to the standard.

Facing page, right: fig. 4 An array of different lamps in St. Giles'

Right: fig. 5 A pre-War lamp near the bridge at Hertford College in New College Lane

Below left: fig. 6 A lamp that appears to grow from the wall, with many mosses and creepers adding to the texture of the stonework

Below right: fig. 7 A lamp by New College wall, clumsily converted, with the old bracket adjacent to it, carelessly left in the masonry to cause probable damage to the wall.

Left: fig. 8 A lollipop lamp that appeared with horrifying suddenness in 1969, but that was replaced with something less offensive. The model was popular at that time.

Right: fig. 9 A lamp in Kybald Street encased within a traditional lantern, and mounted on a new building.

Streetlamps in the years since the War have not been noted for their elegant design, and their intrusion upon the urban scene is far too often visually disastrous. In 1969 and 1970 St. Giles' had a series of lamp-posts down the middle of the road (fig. 4). No fewer than *four* different types of lampfitting were fixed to the tops of the standards. This provided visual anarchy, and it is tragic that our sophisticated and expensive planning machinery was either unable or unwilling to do anything about it. This visual disruption is quite inexcusable, and is especially worrying in the centre of Oxford.

Walking down the Broad to New College Lane, the observer could pass under the bridge at Hertford and find quite decent pre-War lamps of a traditional pattern consisting of Windsor-type lanterns on cast-iron standards (fig. 5). Indeed, the whole stretch of subtle and enclosed streetscape that forms New College Lane and Queen's Lane possesses a number of traditional lamps. These were never disruptive visually, and indeed add to the qualities of the Lane.

There were delightful examples of lamps that appeared to grow from the old wall by All Souls, with many mosses and creepers adding to the character of the scene (fig. 6). Another lamp on its traditional bracket sprang from New College Wall, contrasting with another lantern that had been clumsily converted to electricity, the old bracket having been destroyed in the process (fig. 7).

The crunch comes, however, when the beginnings of erosion are noted. A particularly nasty lamp suddenly appeared on a wall in 1969, and demonstrated to what depths streetlamp design had sunk (fig. 8). Crude, insensitive, ugly, and ill-suited to its environment, it stuck out like some obscene lollipop from the wall. There was no sense here of the lamp's growing out of the wall; no easy repose; and no feeling of sympathy for Oxford. Instead, the new lamp (which doubtless emitted its required lumens with admirable efficiency) was plonked on the wall with singular lack of tact. What was worse was that the City proposed to replace *all* the lamps in the lanes with this monstrous lamp-fitting. Furthermore, we were told at the time that the Fine Art Commission had no objection to the removal of the old lamps. All this appeared to stem from the requirements of street-lighting standards and from the wish of the local authority to standardise its equipment to conform. Some environmentalists, puzzled by this, asked why it was necessary to have bright lighting to suit ideal standards in such a subtle area as the Lanes. The Lanes are not major highways, and are exceedingly pleasant as walks. Cars do have headlamps, and it was suggested politely that new lamps were both unnecessary from the practical as well as from the aesthetic point of view.

In Kybald Street, the new Corpus Christi building had a new electric lamp fixed to a passable bracket attached to the new wall. The lamp was encased within a traditionally-patterned case, and looked civilised. If it could be done there, why, it was asked, could it not be done in the Lanes (fig. 9)?

The outcry was immense, and the lollipop was removed. There is no excuse for ugliness, especially in Oxford, and many people resent paying for the perpetuation, perpetration, and increase of ugliness. The little details as well as the larger objects, such as buildings, add to or detract from the qualities of our physical environment.

Walls are popular things to demolish. Not very long ago a street in Summertown was ruined because a wall was removed. A very decent high wall which was covered in creepers was knocked down (figs. 10, 11). Apart from the fact that a playground for children was formed behind the wall so that neither noise nor balls can be contained, the visual

Left: fig. 10   A street in Summertown, showing the walled character.

Right: fig. 11   The ugly new wall and loss of enclosure

Above left: fig. 12 Magpie Lane looking north, showing the tree and St. Mary's spire before the new Corpus building was erected.

Above right: fig. 13 'Narrow streets, enclosed alleys . . . have qualities of excellence, pleasant proportions, and a sympathetic scale that always soothes the eye'.

Below left: fig. 14 Part of the old city wall, where the lamp casts its shadow on a summer's day.

qualities of the street have been badly damaged. It is as though a 'tooth' had been removed in the frontage. There is no sense in removing a wall which not only did a job of containment, but also looked well. The plates show the character of the street as it was, and as it is now. The fine tree in the background, (damaged during demolition of the wall and of an old house which formerly stood on the site) has been removed. Some new planting, however, has helped.

Trees are important in towns (fig. 12). North Oxford has much of its wonderful qualities because the much-maligned Victorians had the decency to plant trees for posterity. We are now enjoying, or destroying, the trees they planted which are now mature. One ventures to ask what we are doing for our great-grandchildren, but unfortunately the bare and dreary post-war housing estates appear to be the best we can do.

Under recent legislation, local authorities are empowered to plant trees to improve the environment or to require that trees be planted as a condition of planning consent. Thousands of trees should be planted now in the deserts of Oxford's suburbs, to soften the harshness of concrete and of brick. The High would lose much if its magnificent tree between Queen's and All Souls were to go (see chap. 3, fig. 39), while there are other examples in the lanes between Merton Street and the High (see chap. 2, figs. 25, 26). Narrow streets, enclosed alleys, and agreeable buildings have qualities of excellence, pleasant proportions, and a sympathetic scale that always soothes the eye (fig. 13). More planting is needed, and quickly, for the trees the Victorians planted are growing old and many will have to be felled. They must be replaced.

It is the collective effects of these many vandalisms, small tragedies in themselves, that add up to the erosion of the city and the squandering of its heritage. Once, not so long ago, it was a beautiful place. It would be interesting to know *why* it is being wrecked, and how much is it costing to destroy it.

Lamps, road signs and little *nuances* of the visual scene are very important, but there is a need for selective consideration of one or two aspects of the townscape because of the lessons they can teach us.

Oxford is a place of evocations and of delicate visual memory. There is little of the overpowering here: instead, there are the glimpses of images caught between frames or in alleyways. There is nothing of sumptuous grandeur, but an immense richness of ever-changing cameos caught, as it were, in the camera of the mind: the old town wall, for example, casting its shadow on a summer day against a rendered wall, framed by the leaves of a tree, and carrying its lamp (fig. 14). This picture would be very much less interesting without the lamp.

The power of the Church is incomparably expressed in Oxford, and provides points of architectural focus wherever you look (see chap. 2, fig. 23), in the most subtle of ways, without any sense of pomposity or of being overbearing (fig. 15). The church of SS. Philip and James, in North Oxford, stands in an oasis of tree-lined walks and tall Victorian houses, a landmark from the distance and a central focus to the area (fig. 16). As such, it is not only an architectural centre of gravity in a largely domestic mass of development, but it has a social significance as well. It was designed by George Edmund Street and dates from 1862.

These are strong dominants, but there are gentler, less definable foci of the poorer areas. In St. Ebbe's, for example, now laid waste,

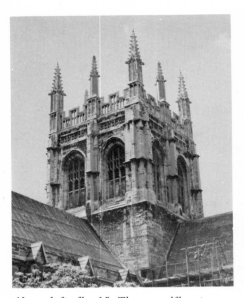

Above left: fig. 15 The magnificent tower of Merton College Chapel

Above right: fig. 16 George Edmund Street's Church of SS. Philip and James (1862) in North Oxford.

Below: fig. 17 Blomfield's Church of St. Barnabas, the campanile of which dominates Jericho. The Bakers Arms can also be seen, distinguished from the houses, only by its lettering.

one or two little pubs still stand (or did at the time of writing), centres of much social activity, and situated, in the best Victorian fashion, on corners. The Albion, a decent unpretentious pub, with good lettering in the vernacular, and traditional St. Ebbe's brick detailing, was a welcome sight among the wasteland as it sported its old brewing signs. Sadly it is now lying derelict. The Royal Blenheim, in St. Ebbe's Street, is a splendidly rich cornerpiece adding much to the townscape. It turns the corner magnificently and the fine scale of the building acts as a 'stop' to the street (see chap. 5, figs. 19, 20).

Down in Jericho, another under-rated part of Oxford architecturally, the area is dominated by the great bulk and tower of Blomfield's St. Barnabas, as good an essay in Victorian church architecture as found anywhere (fig. 17). In Jericho too, the corner pub is much in evidence, and here the scale is purely domestic. The Bakers Arms, for example, is distinguished only by its lettering; not by its architecture.

In Osney Town, a similar area exists with two dominants: the great church of St. Frideswide, and the water. The industrial buildings by the water (fig. 18) are magnificent of their type, with their strong arched brickwork contrasting with the lighter bricks of the walls, while the domestic buildings have an almost rural setting. Again, corner pubs provide foci for communal life, and the architectural quality of the area, so far comparatively undisturbed, needs careful treatment, especially since so many inappropriate windows and doors are being inserted.

Let us consider the stretch of water from Osney Town to Folly Bridge. First of all, there is the wonderful old cast-iron bridge, designed in the City Engineer's department over eighty years ago, and now carrying far more traffic than it was ever intended to take. This valuable and pleasing old structure *must* be saved, for it contributes much to the character of Osney Town (fig. 19). Note the balustrade, spoiled a little

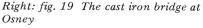

Left: fig. 18 Industrial buildings by the water at Osney Town

Right: fig. 19 The cast iron bridge at Osney

Top: fig. 20 Two domestic buildings in an almost rural setting

Above: fig. 21 A derelict warehouse

Left: fig. 22 The restored warehouse and Maltings

104

Fig. 23: Recent housing at Headington Quarry, where traditional values are respected.

now because the ornamental lamps were removed from the stone piers. If this bridge could be spared its heavy loadings, then it would no doubt suffice, but if it has to be replaced, then it could be re-erected in the Parks, for foot traffic only. It was designed in Oxford in the 1880s, and I think it is a particularly fine example of its type. It should be saved, otherwise its loss will be just another phase in the Erosion of Oxford.

Just downstream, two particularly likeable little houses catch the eye, and, growing from their bankside trees and bushes, are singularly attractive (fig. 20). The lock area has several good features, including excellent and appropriate planting, but it is a source of worry to contemplate the ruined old building south of the lock. Potentially, this is a wonderful structure, with its massive brick walls in the best industrial vernacular tradition punctured by small, well-proportioned openings. Good robust wall tie-ends decorate the façade, and it is to be hoped that this building could be put to beneficial use (fig. 21), as has another former derelict building, also by the water, now converted to good use by the University Surveyor. The old maltings in Tidmarsh Lane are now the offices of the Surveyor and his staff. A few years ago they were literally derelict, and are comparable with the old buildings at Osney. The sensitive and delightfully handled conversion has not altered the character of the building at all, and it is a pleasure to view it either from Fisher Row or from the Lane (fig. 22). Even when new windows have been added, the new work does not obtrude.

It is saddening, not to mention alarming, that so many of the things which make our environment delightful and interesting seem to be ignored by the people engaged in creating the surroundings for modern life. There are exceptions, of course, such as the development in Headington Quarry (fig. 23), which seems to provide enclosure, delicacy, and good proportions with a respect for the site, for nature, and for the existing character of the area.

In other chapters I discuss some of those recent developments which do none of these things, but which seem to epitomise visual ugliness in a way which would lead us to believe that the lessons of Oxford as a beautiful city have been entirely ignored.

5

The Destruction
of St. Ebbe's

'The King to Oxford sent a troop of horse,
For Tories own no argument but force:
With equal skill to Cambridge books he sent,
For Whigs admit no force but argument.'

Sir William Browne:
Nichols's Literary Anecdotes,
vol. ii, p.330
(A reply to Joseph Trapp's version)

*Facing page: Nos. 8-10 Charles
Street, St. Ebbe's*

Cities and towns are subtle things: they need care and gentleness in the ways in which they are treated. Wholesale flattening of great areas is no answer to the problem of decay or obsolescence.

It used to be fashionable among members of the dental profession to remove all or most of a person's teeth and to replace them with artificial, false teeth. Fortunately for our mouths a policy of repair and conservation has replaced the cruder methods of yesteryear. Unfortunately for our towns and cities, policies of 'comprehensive redevelopment' have prevailed which means total obliteration of an area backed up by compulsory purchase and all the other bureaucratic machinery which we are told is for our own good. Movement towards rehabilitation, replacement and repair is gaining ground in enlightened circles, for the qualities that make towns pleasant cannot be created overnight. Enlightenment, however, had not yet dawned when Oxford decided to obliterate St. Ebbe's.

St. Ebbe's was the area bounded by St. Aldate's, Queen Street, the river and the Castle area. It is therefore the south-western quarter of the city. It was a community of narrow streets of terrace houses, small in scale, with corner shops, pubs, small businesses, and a strong sense of community. It was known officially as a slum area, yet many of the houses were kept meticulously. The very designation of the term 'slum' reflects a middle-class attitude to terrace-housing where grand values are applied to humble situations.

St. Ebbe's had its own life and industry. The gasworks, the brewery, the canal and various businesses were important sources of employment. As well as providing architectural foci, they were social and employment centres.

St. Ebbe's has been destroyed. For years a whole part of Oxford near the City's heart, part of its ancient settlement pattern, part of its history and life, has lain broken and derelict, empty and hideous as the result of a misguided official policy. Now a road layout which has no resemblance to any over-all plan for the area has been built. It will be well nigh impossible to plan the place as a unit, because the roads have been planned first and the spaces in between will be filled in afterwards. This is no way to plan. The spaces so created are known as SLOAP (Space Left Over After Planning).

Published plans showed a row of seventeenth-century houses in Charles Street (renamed Turn Again Lane) to be retained (fig. 1). The terrace had been allowed to fall into disrepair. An architect bought the middle house and restored it in such a way that it became a desirable dwelling. He repaired the house by his own efforts and expertise. As his family expanded he needed more room, so what more natural than to try and buy the property next door, which was structurally sound but otherwise needed immediate attention to *prevent* it from *becoming* unsound?

The legal owner sold to the Council and the architect tried to buy from the Council. However, they would only give him leasehold, and that for a very short term, which would have made it a poor proposition for him to put capital into the property to repair it and make it inhabitable. The architect had tried to buy from the owner, but the owner refused as, if he sold privately, his rights to be re-housed would be forfeited.

The architect, seeing that the Council had little intention of

keeping to its officially declared policy in its published plans and
statements, realised that the whole terrace was likely to be doomed.
He sold out to the Council as the value of his property (part of the
terrace as a *whole*, architecturally and historically) was bound to
drop as it would have been the only 'tooth' left in the emptiness.

The saga of the houses in Charles Street is almost unbelievable.
Late in 1968, the Corporation decided to demolish two houses (nos.
6 and 7) in Charles Street on the grounds that a new sewer, about to
be laid for the Westgate shopping centre, would be so near the houses
that there would be a danger of the houses collapsing on the men
digging the trench! The Central Area Redevelopment Committee
authorised the demolition, as the houses were alleged to be 'dangerous'.
Environmentalists protested that it was a sad reflection of the
Corporation's engineering skill that it was necessary to demolish the
houses to prevent their collapsing into a new drain.

It was said at the time that the houses were vital ingredients in
the pretty Charles Street row, and that if they went, there would be
little hope for the remainder of the street, which would suffer the
same dusty fate as Paradise Square. The recommendation to pull the
houses down was accepted by the Planning Committee as well as
by the Central Area Redevelopment Committee, despite the fact
that the Consultants' Central Area Study showed Charles Street
intact, and that, during the 1965 public inquiry, the City Architect

*Fig. 1: Nos. 8-10 Charles Street, St. Ebbe's. No. 8, to the left of the photo, was
restored by an architect for his own habitation. Nos. 6 and 7, which once adjoined
No. 8, are no more. These three seventeenth-century houses are basically all that is
left of historic St. Ebbe's apart from Paradise Street and the area in the shadow of the
castle.*

and Planning Officer said the street would be preserved if possible. Needless to say, the houses were Listed as of Architectural and Historic Interest.[1] The editorial comment in the *Oxford Mail* emphasised the importance of the fact that it was intended to get rid of the houses before proper publicity had been given, and before any alternative was costed. 'There should not be one rule for the council and another for private developers. The intention to destroy any house listed as of architectural interest . . . ought to be made public before action is taken.'[2]

The houses were demolished.

The sequel was boringly predictable. Only a year later, pressure mounted to demolish the remaining three houses, Nos. 8–10. The then Council, which owned No. 9, decided to buy No. 8 (the architect's house) and No. 10 (occupied by an elderly couple).[3] The Council was 'anxious that the area should be redeveloped soon'. That was in 1969. Environmentalists were alerted. The Civic Society, the Oxford Preservation Trust, and the Oxford Architectural and Historical Society were ready this time. On 11 December, J. R. L. Highfield, President of the Oxford Architectural and Historical Society, expressed his 'grave concern' that the 'preservation of 8, 9, and 10 Charles Street' had 'been called into question' by the then Chairman of the Central Area Redevelopment Committee.

'Is it really for the present generation planners to dissipate the wealth of our architectural heritage in Oxford and thus to incur the consequent odium which will be felt by those who come after us?' asked Dr. Highfield, before putting an eloquent case for conservation. In the same issue of the *Oxford Mail*[4] Adytum also spoke out about the proposals, putting the case more bluntly than Dr. Highfield.[4]

The Chairman of the Central Area Redevelopment Committee predictably replied, and provoked a response from Gerard L'Estrange Turner, then Hon. Secretary of the Oxford Civic Society. Mr. Turner pointed out that part of our national heritage was being sacrificed to finance. If we look more closely at what was said at the time about finance, however, we find that the need for economy was due to the fact that large areas of the city centre lay derelict. If we examine the way in which it was proposed to maintain the heritage of Oxford, we see that this was to be done by getting the road proposals accepted.

These two points put together in a nutshell what is, and has for years been wrong with the fundamental planning policy. Out of the devastated area in St. Ebbe's — to make way for 'the road' and commercial development — only about one sixth was even potentially a source of rateable income.

Historic Oxford has been carved up to serve that very doubtful god, the private car. The consultants' plan hardly mentions the potential of public transport, but even in the U.S.A., restriction of the car in cities and extension of public transport is gaining powerful support.

Mr. Turner pointed out that St. Ebbe's could have been substantially retained as a most valuable residential counterpoise to the colleges. No such balance is provided by the hotch-potch of commercial development and public buildings, divided by roads and car-parks, which seems to be the present fate of St. Ebbe's.

A city council takes expert advice from its permanent officials, but it is bound to follow the clearly expressed wishes of the citizens.

In the same issue[5], Adytum also counter-attacked in a letter which answered the Chairman's various points.

The Council and its officials have claimed to be responsible for the planning and redevelopment of the city and they were said to have worked hard to get the *road and traffic proposals accepted*, but this in itself was a source of great concern, for it demonstrates the kind of piecemeal and meaningless planning which bedevils the city, contributing more than any other factor to the Erosion of Oxford.

The 'public' needs a decent environment in which to live healthy lives. I do not consider a sea of tarmac laid over a destroyed community to be contributory to 'improved road facilities' and to 'educational and welfare services'. The Council pleaded for the 'exercise' of 'responsibility in planning' and 'in the finances of Oxford'. Piece-meal planning unrelated to any over-all conception, the destruction of property with rateable value, and the leaving of a huge acreage waste over several years is not indicative of either responsible action or a modicum of sense.

The last remaining vestiges of old St. Ebbe's were in danger, despite the assurances by the City after the 1963 Review that they would be conserved, and they were threatened by the very body charged with good planning responsibility. Chain stores and pompous monuments to municipal power do not seem to fit the local authority's categories of responsible management of either finance or planning powers.

True to form, on 9 January 1970 the *Oxford Times* reported that the City Council was to seek Ministry approval for the demolition of the three seventeenth-century houses in Charles Street, despite impassioned pleas from conservationists and from sympathetic councillors, one of whom called the proposed destruction of the houses 'civic vandalism'.

On 30 January 1970, it was reported[6] that £1,250 had been offered for No. 10 Charles Street by the Council. The old couple who lived there wanted to remain in St. Ebbe's. The developers, however, were offering £8,500 for this site with the houses, and £35,000 for the site provided they could be demolished. Since the council voted to demolish, the site value alone would appear to be considerably higher than the ludicrously small sum offered to the old couple.

The campaign continued, and to everyone's relief, the three houses are still standing, though in a dreadful setting. The Oxford Preservation Trust stepped in and stymied the Council on the question of a 'viable use' which, it was alleged, would be difficult to find. The Trust simply offered to establish its offices in the houses. The outcry was so concerted and vigorously pursued that the Council was forced to admit the strength of the conservationist case. Pressure from amenity groups did work, and it was clearly not a waste of time writing to the papers, or agitating. Oxford can have cause to be profoundly grateful to the three groups who so vehemently opposed the Council. The Trust is to be especially thanked for its splendid gesture in establishing itself in Charles Street.

Not far from these remaining parts of seventeenth-century Oxford was the Gardener's Arms, a splendid little 'local' that, only a few years ago, resounded to happy laughter and was the haunt of agreeable company. In 1968 it was reduced to an empty shell and flattened (fig. 2).

Left: fig. 2 The shell of the Gardeners Arms, formerly a most attractive traditional pub, with good ale and food.

Facing page, above: fig. 3 The approach to Folly Bridge showing the entrance to St. Ebbe's from St. Aldate's

Facing page, below: fig. 4 '. . . huge open windswept areas of car park'

Erosion on a large scale has resulted in the almost total removal of St. Ebbe's. A structureless area is left where all is confusion, and orientation is impossible. The Council has built roads without having a coherent plan for the area.

The access and egress points to this tortuous part of Oxford which consists only of roads and car parks are dismal in the extreme. Fig. 3 shows a typical highway engineer's scheme just north of Folly Bridge. Round the corner a new road ploughs its way to the centre of the wilderness. The lighting authorities have ensured that the ugly scene will not be shrouded in merciful darkness.

Development in St. Ebbe's seems to consist largely of huge open windswept areas of car park (fig. 4) and buildings of mediocre quality. The Telephone Exchange in Speedwell Street must be numbered among the ugliest buildings in Britain (fig. 5). It displays such a total lack of feeling for the scale of Oxford, as well as stark lack of sensibility in itself that one despairs for the future environment. The monstrous bulk of the telephone building, whereon a great number of materials has been indiscriminately used, augurs ill for any future for the qualities of the area. This is a crude piece of work, if ever there was one. Rubble, brick, concrete, glass, colour and forms jar and offend the eye. The sheer weight of the thing makes its point with brutal force, and betrays the soulless nature of an impersonal bureaucratic authority that can perpetrate such an outrage in Oxford or anywhere else.

The enormity of the aesthetic crime from the scale point of view is doubly hammered home when we see the problem of the juxtaposition of the Magistrates' Courts. Clearly, every effort has been made to make this basically small building appear bigger, but somehow

112

it just has not worked. The elevation of this building to Speedwell Street is not entirely happy, but we must thank the restorers of Alice's shop for the charming vignettes which we find looking through an archway past a balcony and over to the main front of the Courts. Nothing, however, can alleviate the crudity of the telephone building. It dominates the whole of St. Ebbe's and the spirit wilts in the face of such an assault on feeling.

The other building occupied by the telephone authorities, in Paradise Street, clearly owes no allegiance to the intimate qualities of the area (fig. 6). If a walk is taken down Titmouse Lane (re-named by the puritans as 'Tidmarsh' presumably because of an aversion from rodents) past the excellent conversion of the old Malt House (fig. 7), over Quaking Bridge and past the ruined Castle, the spirit sinks to the depths of gloom again. The stream under St. George's Tower is a foul mess, filled with bottles and rubbish.

Squalor does not end here, however, for dismal sights such as that in fig. 8 are not uncommon, while the Oxpens Road recreation ground displays a lack of imagination.

It is all the more gloomy, therefore, to have to turn to part of

Facing page, above: fig. 5 The brutal telephones building in Speedwell Street.

Facing page, below left: fig. 6 Office buildings in Paradise Street

Facing page, below right: fig. 7 A sympathetic new use for an old building: the University Surveyor's Offices in the Old Maltings.

Below: fig. 8 Semi-dereliction in St. Ebbe's

Fig. 9: New housing is unrelated to the river. The Telephones building is on the right.

St. Ebbe's which has been redeveloped for a proper purpose, namely
as housing. It is sad to have to see it as a missed opportunity. The
river is pleasant here, and yet the new housing is unrelated with the
river (fig. 9). Not only is it unrelated with the water, but there seems
no over-all concept for the watersides on *both* banks. The housing is
seen over acres of waste land, littered with weeds, bottles, old shoes,
rubbish and general unpleasantness. It is not really good enough,
and what is potentially a marvellous site seems to have been misjudged. Fig. 10 shows the sort of thing which is disturbing: too much
of the open space is unkempt and waste; the bridge, a pleasant
structure, is not being used, although it would provide an admirable
link to the opposite shore.

We misuse our rivers. We do not make anything of them. We
waste a potential resource. This housing could have been exciting,
with riverside walks, pubs, and little alleyways leading down to the
waterfront. Any one of Oxford's riverside pubs is an object-lesson
for us here, and surely it would sink into someone's head that a
riverside pub in *central* Oxford would be a tremendous asset!

As it is, the quality of the open space is simply dreary. Look at
the industrial mess in Fig. 10, which shows how badly Oxford treats its
riverside. The waste lands, the litter, the ugly fencing, all combine to
make an unpardonable blot on the landscape.

Spaces and landscaping recently completed have not been fully
successful. The grass is long and unkempt. The fiddly little patches of
earth are not used and look untidy. The tree planting is unimaginative

and too sparse. Bollards appear for no apparent reason (fig. 11). It might have been better to have constructed these houses using fewer materials and requiring less maintenance. There appear to be huge areas of painted timber boarding which need painting at regular intervals. Coloured panels, bricks, timber, tiles and so on create a restless effect and are far too fussy.

Bricks could have been used throughout, as was the tradition in St. Ebbe's, and the money saved on maintenance could then have gone to more landscaping and better maintenance of it. Probably separate funds exist for both painting and landscape maintenance, and the bureaucratic barriers would not permit any overlap, but from a logical point of view it all seems rather questionable.

If ever there were a case for asking for an overall plan for St. Ebbe's it has been made by the extraordinary way in which the Council has acted over the bridge linking Grandpont and St. Ebbe's. Only a few years ago they wanted to demolish it, but changed their minds when it was pointed out that it might be desirable to walk from the residential area in Grandpont to St. Ebbe's instead of having to walk all the way to Folly Bridge. Meanwhile, the skeletal bridge still lacks a walkway at the time of writing, and is of no use as yet to the people who live nearby. The few dwellings which the Council has erected are again constructed of far too many materials, many of which will require expensive maintenance if appearances are to be kept up. The garish colours do not help either, especially in such a subtle situation as that provided by Thameside (fig. 12). For some reason which defies analysis, the Council

Fig. 10: Industrial dereliction and mess

Fig. 11: All the coloured panels, bricks, timber, tiling, and so on create a fussy effect. The landscaping and new planting are not successful either.

Fig. 12: The disused bridge: a potential link between Grandpont and St. Ebbe's. Note the materials used in the new flats that will require considerable maintenance.

ignores the traditional materials used by the river. These consist of good red and yellow brickwork, timber, and some stone, although the latter is not common by the riverside. Instead of learning from the traditions, the Council has imposed its own brand of arrogance on the river bank in the form of the totally foreign brown bricks, pastel-shaded panels and far too much white paint. Elsewhere in St. Ebbe's the same mistakes are being repeated, where weak, flabby colours are being used in the College of Further Education instead of a good traditional St. Ebbe's red brick (fig. 13). Here was a case where a building was designed in phases, the newer blocks hardly relating at all to the original pavilions.

Look at the old buildings along by the banks of the river near Folly Bridge (fig. 14). These could be adapted as clubs, pubs or housing, and would be superbly situated. To reiterate the point made previously, we must not waste the river, one of our greatest assets.

Incidentally, note on the left of the picture that the iron balustrade has been filled in with chicken wire. This looks very tatty indeed, and those responsible should note that there are hundreds of other places where children could fall in the water, and if they want to they will. In Holland, there are not railings everywhere by canal banks, but the mortality rate due to drowning is not exceptionally high there. There are far too many people who wish to protect us from ourselves in this country, and the results are glaring street-lamps, a profusion of bad signs and chicken wire, fencing and posts everywhere. They all contribute to the increase of ugliness, and this ugliness can and must be avoided.

The possibility that a massive hotel may soon be built on the banks of the river is horrifying, for not only will the human scale of the river bank be lost, but the possibility of forming a walk will be squandered. Now there is nothing worse than a dreary riverside walk of the character of the south bank. Unsoftened by trees or by any mysterious openings between buildings, the walk is an unimaginative sweep. The

Left: fig. 13 Part of the College of Further Education. This building is an attempt to superimpose order on St. Ebbe's, but has been spoiled by the use of light buff bricks and by later additions.

Below: fig. 14 Buildings by the riverside

Fig. 15: Folly Bridge and the marvellous Folly building

same thing could happen to the northern bank, with great loss to the character of the river. Folly Bridge, with the marvellous old Folly itself (fig. 15), is a splendid example of how Oxford's river could appear. The house rises up from the waters, and balconies of elegant ironwork permit flowers and creepers to trail downwards. Lichens and mosses grow on the sun-soaked walls, and the whole composition is unforgettable and delightful. You do not have to destroy all this to get a riverside walk, for the walk can sometimes go *behind* the buildings, so that the river is sometimes directly by the path, and sometimes is not. How much more interesting is Wapping High Street than the South Bank in London! Oxford must learn that her riverside needs care and subtle attention, not crudity of thought and action. With horror we contemplate the thought of the huge hotels proposed for the Folly Bridge area, and with despair we hear the opinion of an official of the Council who thought that one of them could be designed as a unit with a large car-park! Such a view demonstrates that the official in question did not understand the first thing about scale nor about the scale in particular of Oxford.

Our riverside, like our city, is a precious inheritance. We have damaged it badly, and we have desecrated the collective creative legacy of our predecessors. Let us not abuse the opportunity presented by the Thames, rather let us show that we are capable of caring. The admirable publication, *Oxford's Waterways*, produced in 1974 by the Oxford Waterways Action Group, a joint working-party of the Oxford Civic Society and the Oxford Preservation Trust, analyses the waterways situation admirably and makes some excellent recommendations.

Although much has happened to cause despair for the future quality of the environment of Oxford, disasters such as the flattening of St. Ebbe's, and the efforts of the highway authorities who seem to assume that all motorists are either morons or suffering from vision defects, a few reasonable things have been done.

It is good, for example, to see the restoration of Alice's shop, although it seems to have been more of a rebuilding than a restoration. Certainly the view from the Memorial Gardens (fig. 16) would be all the poorer had the building been demolished, although it is now largely obscured by the unfortunate 'Bridewell Square' redevelopment. A jaundiced look is spared for the 'temporary' shops in St. Aldate's (fig. 17). Readers will probably remember the old houses that used to stand on this site, and that contributed much more positively to the urban townscape than this single-storey affair. Incidentally, the houses contained murals featuring several subsequently celebrated undergraduates of the twenties. A mess of advertisements and a 'forecourt'

Fig. 16: Alice's Shop, St. Aldate's

littered with six nasty little seats, it does not add anything of quality
to the streets of Oxford. It would be interesting to see how much it
would have cost compared with these shops to have built permanent
shops with, say, housing over them. It is debateable how temporary
is 'temporary' in this context.

Almost opposite, a delightful little view is had of a narrow court
off St. Aldate's. It goes to show what can be done with imagination
and a little trouble. The sunlight is caught in a tiny paved area in
which plants grow in ordered profusion. It is a pleasure to see, and it
would be marvellous to see more such agreeable things in Oxford
(fig. 18).

I wonder how many people who go about their daily lives in
Oxford actually notice those little details of the fabric of the city
which combine to form that overall quality which saves Oxford from
disagreeable bareness.

Remember The Albion, once an unpretentious little pub at the
bottom of Littlegate Street. It was nothing more than a typical mid-
nineteenth century corner house of cheap red brick, but was
enlivened by corbelled brickwork at the gutter line made of different
bricks, and the well-proportioned window was made that small
amount grander by the addition of painted voussoirs over the window.
The plaque which celebrated the name of the pub is simple, bold and
irrefutably decent. The chimney was treated in an interesting manner,
with the corners picked out in yellow bricks (fig. 19).

Just up the street in St. Ebbe's Street itself is the late nineteenth-
century Royal Blenheim, a composition with gabled roof and façades

122

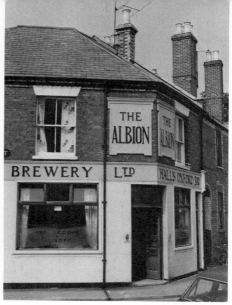

Facing page: fig. 17 'Temporary' shops in St. Aldate's on the site of some splendid old buildings.

Above left: fig. 18 A courtyard in St. Aldate's

Above right: fig. 19 The Albion in St. Ebbe's as it was.

Right: fig. 20 The Royal Blenheim

of great interest, turning the corner with subtle aplomb into the side street.

Of particular note are the ground-floor windows, very charmingly detailed: the plaque with ornamental cartouche on the wall in St. Ebbe's Street; and the delicious mixture of Arts and Crafts tile hanging with half-timbered first floor. This pub building is an object lesson in how to build up a corner site with elegance and with style. Other examples occur at Carfax, where both the Midland Bank and Lloyds sit very happily on their corners.

A study of the Blenheim, however, reveals the good articulation of the design (fig. 20). Viewed from the south, the design is even better, for here the gables add a note of lightness to a street now sadly made lumpish by the crudity of the City Chambers, an essay if ever there was one on how *not* to treat a corner site. Note how the Blenheim's chimney rises up from the gables in a picturesque and pleasing composition.

Fig. 21: The vicarage of St. Thomas. A beautiful building combining a vernacular style with Gothic detail.

Talking of gables, the charming vicarage of St. Thomas's also provides an example of subtle use of architectural forms (fig. 21). The lovely late-Victorian Gothic treatment of the blind panels above the entrance door is a delight, while the whole building sits unobtrusively and solidly beside the agreeable old church.

Gables appear again at Morrell's Brewery near St. Thomas's, treated with less sureness this time, but our eyes are attracted by the entrance gates of iron (fig. 22). The name of the brewery is carried in a great segmental arch of iron supported on two light yet strong gateposts topped by cast-iron lions gilded. This is an object of excellence, and is one of the last pleasures in an area which has been treated barbarously.

Fairly near the Brewery, we find Fisher Row, a street of almost eighteenth-century calm. The houses are well mannered and discreet, while the iron railings, old cast-iron lamp standards, narrow walkways and the proximity of fine mature trees and the water create an enclave of great beauty (fig. 23).

In St. Ebbe's, in part of the old development not yet flattened at the time of writing, a sad comment on the times is found (fig. 24). A

Above: fig. 22 Morrell's Brewery

Right: fig. 23 Fine old houses in Fisher Row

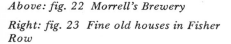

charming old gas lamp at the corner of Trinity Street stands somewhat dejectedly in the deserted and weed-covered pavement. A traditional street-nameplate is fixed to the wall in a simple and satisfactory manner. Like the lamp, it is constructed of cast iron, and it is of course too much to ask the Council to stick to this type of nameplate. The lettering is bold and simple, and the design is easy on the eye. Compare it with the visually weak sign below where the type-face has not even been accurately rendered.

The old Victorian tenements look quite attractive in the sunlight photographed from beneath the trees which used to line the walk to St. Thomas's Recreation Ground (fig. 25). They are interesting examples of nineteenth-century mass-housing and are rare in Oxford although very common in London's East End. Structurally, they appear very sound, and presumably could be up-graded by a re-organisation of the insides to bring them up to standard. It might be necessary to knock two apartments into one and to do something with the vertical circulation but with some imagination they could become very attractive houses. You only have to walk round the corner to see what the University Surveyor has done with the old Malt House to see that sound old buildings can be re-adapted for modern needs in a wholly satisfactory way, and that they should not be thoughtlessly destroyed.

Our heritage is being eroded. Will there be anything left for our children to enjoy, or will they be condemned to live in a tree-less, quality-less environment which is overlit by night so that there is never any escape?

A word of warning is necessary about St. Ebbe's and Littlegate

Left: fig. 24 A traditional corner in old St. Ebbe's

Right: fig. 25 Victorian tenements in St. Thomas's. These are fine and substantial buildings and owe not a little to Butterfield and Ruskin.

Streets. No doubt the temptation to destroy by road-widening was great in the 1960s, but the street is an object-lesson in enclosure and visual 'stops' which must not be ignored. The pleasing old vicarage with its walled garden at the rear of the Albion, for example, is one of Oxford's best buildings of the genre (fig. 26).

I wonder, too, at the wisdom of proceeding with such a large traffic-generating scheme as the Westgate without the roads to take the increase. There is no point in saying the road network in *St. Ebbe's* will improve things, for it is the *access to those roads themselves* which is important. It is as though Westgate was built to ensure the need for the roads of the future. As if to prevent a mass of traffic from penetrating the remains of Charles Street, the absurd lengths to which we have to resort were captured for ever by the camera lens in 1970 (fig. 27). Such pearls add humour to a serious situation, but demonstrate to what lengths we have allowed the requirements of the motor car to impinge upon our urban fabric.

Old St. Ebbe's was a living community (fig. 28). Today it is a wilderness of ugliness. Paradise Square at the turn of the century was a

Right: fig. 26 The old vicarage of St. Ebbe's in Littlegate Street.

Left: fig. 27 The absurd lengths to which we have resorted to prevent the traffic from penetrating Charles Street, now appropriately named Turn Again Lane. Although ephemeral, the picture makes its point.

Below: fig. 28 Old St. Ebbe's

Fig. 29: Paradise Square, St. Ebbe's, as it was in the 1890s. Note the beautifully-kept vegetable garden and the decent houses in the square.

Fig. 30: Paradise Square today

Fig. 31: A view from Paradise Street looking towards the Westgate development.
Fig. 32: The pedestrian is driven underground by the City Council.

charming place (fig. 29). Today, it has lost that charm (fig. 30). This is typical of the disastrous erosion that has occurred in the humbler parts of the city. The view past the Jolly Farmers and other fine old buildings in St. Ebbe's towards the new Westgate development emphasises the change of scale between old and new (fig. 31). The emphasis on motor-cars is apparent from fig. 32, for pedestrians are driven into dismal, ugly underground passages. It is this dehumanising of the environment in the name of 'progress' (that doctrine, as Baudelaire observed, of idlers and Belgians) that is all the more distressing when it is realised what has been lost.

Attempts have been made to create new urban spaces. St. Ebbe's Church in its new square is more integrated as a building with the fabric of the city, but the architecture of the surrounding buildings lacks panache or beauty (fig. 33). There are also several new buildings in the vicinity of Campion Hall that try, with curved corners, to create a recognisable 'style' (fig. 34). Perhaps the most successful new buildings are those of the Roman Catholic chaplaincy of 1970–1 by Ahrends, Burton, and Koralek (fig. 35). Beautifully detailed, and suitably reticent, these buildings enhance the setting of adjacent structures.

There are a few good buildings, but generally, the story of St. Ebbe's is one of dismal failure in environmental terms.

It is probably too much to hope for that an overall and *coherent* plan for St. Ebbe's will emerge some day soon that will improve on the disasters outlined above. The vision of William Morris, poet, designer and social reformer has gone sour. We have betrayed his hopes for the

Facing page, left: fig. 33 St. Ebbe's in its new setting

Middle: fig. 34 New buildings near Campion Hall

Right: fig. 35 The new Catholic Chaplaincy buildings in St. Ebbe's

clear Thames bordered by its gardens green, while Spenser's *Sweet Thames!* is something almost beyond our recall, like the nostalgia of an eternal Edwardian summer, or the quietness and unpolluted atmosphere of an English evening's *magic hush.*

Oxford has turned away from its river, as if ashamed, letting the waters flow by the nettles, barbed wire, rubbish dumps and the ruins of St. Ebbe's. A great opportunity has been wasted.

[1] *Oxford Mail,* 12 December 1968.
[2] Ibid.
[3] *Oxford Mail,* 5 December 1969.
[4] *Oxford Mail,* 11 December 1969.
[5] *Oxford Mail,* 23 December 1969.
[6] *Oxford Mail,* 30 January 1970.

6

St. Clement's

'The King, observing with judicious eyes
The state of both his universities,
To Oxford sent a troop of horse, and why?
That learned body wanted loyalty;
To Cambridge books, as very well discerning
How much that loyal body wanted learning.'

Joseph Trapp: On George I's
Donation of the Bishop of Ely's
Library to Cambridge University
Nichols's Literary Anecdotes,
vol. iii, p.330

Facing page: fig. 1 New St. Clement's Church

It is not known if the parish of St. Clement's owes its name to that Clemens who was St. Paul's associate and subsequently Bishop of Rome, or to some other Clement of lesser antiquity. The names of early Christian celebrities were perpetuated in many later generations, and a certain telescoping of the time-scale must be expected.

The compact mediaeval city of Oxford was graced by many fine churches, chapels, chantries, and shrines. West of the city was the glorious Abbey of Osney. Oxford has suffered many sorrows and much destruction in her rich and varied past. The first half of the sixteenth century witnessed the worst period in a story of vandalism which has continued in less spectacular bursts since then. The Abbey gave the livings to many parishes in the surrounding countryside, and was as rich in architectural terms as anything which survives within the walls today. The Friaries of St. Ebbe's, the Trinitarians, the Austin Friars, Rewley, and many chantry chapels and shrines were destroyed by the Tudors, and great must have been the anguish of men of sensibility and taste when those incomparable legacies of a great artistic and cultural past were ruthlessly demolished. No sound, no hint of their sorrow, has come down to us, for the power of the king and his new oligarchy was backed by a merciless system which eliminated all traces of opposition.

Oxford retreated within its walls, and, deprived of the institutions

Fig. 2: A view from Magdalen Bridge in Victorian times, looking eastwards towards the Plain. This photograph was taken before the tramlines were laid, and shows the toll-gate and the elegant turnpike offices where the toll-keeper lived. Behind is the old graveyard of St. Clement's.

and buildings that had once made her a great city by mediaeval standards, changed in character. The remaining mediaeval buildings were few, and we must look at Magdalen, New College, Merton, and others as fortunate survivals, remembering they are only representative of a fraction of the glory that was Oxford.

Many churches survived, however, if somewhat stripped of their finery, and some were actually outside the walls. Beyond the northern gates of the city was the church of St. Giles, while immediately to the east was St. Clement's, sited on what is now known as 'The Plain'. It must have been delightful to walk down The High centuries ago, and to leave the confines of the city via the East Gate. The late-Gothic tower of Magdalen College on the left held the eye, as it does today, although the road itself was infinitely more rural, little more than a muddy tract, in fact. Across the Cherwell was the church of St. Clement surrounded by its churchyard. Old St. Clement's was demolished in 1826, and a new church in the Romanesque style was built down near the river on a less commanding site, so that it was no longer such a dominant architectural feature in the heart of the parish (fig. 1). Something of the sense of leaving the city by a gate was preserved until fairly recently. The old Tollgate at The Plain (fig. 2) marked the beginning of St. Clement's proper. A comparison with the same view as it is today demonstrates how far erosion has gone.

Fig. 3: The same view as that shown in fig. 2 as it is today, showing the Wayneflete Building of Magdalen College on the left and the Victorian Fountain.

Fig. 4: The buildings between St. Clement's High Street and Cowley Road '. . . a good example of how unpretentious buildings with vertical emphasis combined to form an excellent group'. But erosion has taken place, for the small, timber-framed building in the centre is no more.

BRITANNIC
ASSURANCE
CO. LTD.

COWLEY ROAD

BRITANNIC ASS

HOUSE
PURCHASE
FIRE

MON-SAT
NO
WAITING

The site of old St. Clement's church and graveyard is now partly occupied by The Plain roundabout, which is redeemed to some extent by the presence of mature trees (fig. 3). The approach to St. Clement's from Oxford is, however, greatly spoiled by the harshness of the Wayneflete building erected by Magdalen. A charming Regency house and several unobtrusive small-scale buildings used to occupy the site of the Wayneflete, and some idea of the former character on the east side of The Plain may still be seen (figs. 2 and 4). Each element is not exactly distinguished, but *en masse* the effect is subtle. The block between St. Clement's High Street and Cowley Road is a good example of how unpretentious buildings with vertical emphases combined to form an excellent group (fig. 4). Especially, the Britannic Assurance building and The Cape of Good Hope on the corners of the beginning of the Cowley Road are notable examples of successfully designed buildings in that the difficult problem posed where irregularly fanning main roads branch off from The Plain has been solved. The gabled façades help to emphasise the verticality and essentially small, domestic, scale, a characteristic of St. Clement's. Unfortunately, the centre of the block between London Road and Cowley Road has been demolished. It is to be hoped that any rebuilding will not disrupt the vertical elements of the composition.

St. Clement's began to grow as a residential suburb of Oxford in the nineteenth century when most of its fabric familiar to us today was built. The characteristic, red brickwork of the two- or three-storey houses, and the High Street which stretches out in a curve towards the bottom of Headington Hill, developed at that time as did its own institutions, shops, pubs and almshouses. With the growth of population, general in the nineteenth century, so St. Clement's became

Fig. 5: The beautiful fin-de-siècle front of the Half Moon

Fig. 6: The Florey Building

prey to epidemics of which there were several in the course of the era. Cholera struck in Oxford and St. Clement's was not spared.

An exploration of St. Clement's can only be accomplished on foot, starting from The Plain. On the left-hand side of London Road (St. Clement's High Street) is the charming Edwardian front of the Half Moon pub, with its glazed bricks and tiles, and a fine window with etched glass (fig. 5). Walking further east, the former Municipal Restaurant appears in a hideous gap in the frontage of the street, and the squalor of the surroundings is very unfortunate. Behind the restaurant is the new university Florey building, definitely a 'one-off' job that owes nothing to its surroundings, and treats St. Clement's with an obvious contempt by ignoring it (fig. 6). The chaotic conditions prevailing in this part of St. Clement's, where a car park creates its own brand of ugliness are lessons in the difficulties of ensuring related and harmonious planning (fig. 7).

To the north-west of St. Clement's is that long, remarkably flat, quiet green space known as the Angel Meadow. To get to this beautiful, mysterious, peaceful place, it is necessary to cross one of the tributaries of the river. A bridge leads enticingly to the sunlit meadow beyond (fig. 8). From the bridge, a view of the backs of houses to Boulter Street shows how well St. Clement's could relate to the natural

Fig. 7: A car-park, near the Municipal Restaurant (to the left of the 'Way Out' sign). The Wayneflete Building dominates the picture on the right.

amenities (fig. 9). A view looking the other way shows the reality: broken-down fencing, and overgrown riverbanks (despite a regular use of the river by people in punts), and the glowering uninteresting bulk of the Wayneflete Building. Yet the walks down to the river from St. Clement's Street are potentially charming.

The Meadow itself is surrounded by trees, and at one end is the elegant stonework of Magdalen Bridge. Magdalen College tower rises majestically over the leaves, and as the eye travels gradually east two jarring notes are struck: the Wayneflete building again, and the great bulk of the glazed façade of the new Florey building. The latter has a greater vertical emphasis than the Wayneflete, but the elements in the new buildings have a great deal of horizontality, as well as sheer bulk, that create uneasy changes. The vertical thrust of Magdalen College is due not only to the magnificent and noble tower, but also to the pinnacles, chimneys, and other features. Yet mediaeval architecture not only has a strong vertical emphasis: it has, above all, *repose* and a sensitivity to *human scale*.

What is equally important in terms of architectural success in the context of Oxford is the use of natural stone, a material that seems to grow from the very soil of Oxford, and which seems to have absorbed the suns of centuries. The bricks of the nineteenth-century St. Clement's were different, but they were generally of a strong enough colour and a rough texture to be able to create something of a local character: you crossed the river, left Oxford, and here was something smaller in scale and humbler. Occasionally, there were stone buildings such as the pubs

Fig. 8: 'A bridge leads enticingly to the sunlit meadow beyond'
Fig. 9: Part of Boulter Street from the bridge in fig. 8

Fig. 10: The Old Black Horse

and the almshouses, but generally the material was a good red brick,
while one or two buildings were of timber-frame structure with lath
and plaster walls. All these materials fused in the fabric, because they
were unpretentious, and because the scale of each individual building
was essentially domestic and did not attempt to be independent. Each
house owed something, even if it were only a party wall, to its neigh-
bour, and architectural good manners were always in evidence. The
new Collegiate buildings are no longer small, domestic units, and the
choice of materials is no longer dictated by what is locally available.
Both buildings have structural frames, clad, infilled according to an
arbitrary aesthetic that has no local roots.

The Old Black Horse opposite is a wonderful survival, and its
cobbled forecourt with the two fine trees is a great potential asset to
St. Clement's (fig. 10). It is a great pity this feature is practically
impossible to use at present because of the traffic conditions in the
High Street. The street is composed for the most part of nineteenth-
century buildings with little shops on the ground floors, and living
accommodation above: just the sort of village street providing a
variety of uses that livens up any town, especially if it is *used* by
people (fig. 11). This sort of thing would be impossible with wholesale
redevelopment, for the little family businesses could not afford the
inflated rents, and therefore the character of this street should be
preserved by a policy of repair and modernisation, not destruction.
Of course, to enable this to be carried out, the traffic problem will
have to be resolved, and it is essential before investment can take
place to get the cars and heavy vehicles out of St. Clement's Street
altogether. The traffic conditions are appalling now.

St. Clement's has a series of *culs-de-sac* and pedestrian walkways which have good, sound brick walls, trees, enclosure, and a pleasant quality. These routes must be preserved and repaired where necessary as an invaluable part of the area in a motor-car-dominated age, where pedestrian routes are needed. They link St. Clement's Street with the Cowley Road, and include Alma Place (an agreeable street of typical local terrace houses), Tyndale Road, and branch off from the Almshouses (figs. 12, 13). Opposite the Almshouses are some potentially enhanceable areas between St. Clement's High Street and the River (fig. 14).

Perhaps the finest group of buildings in St. Clement's, however, is found at the bottom of Headington Hill. London Place consists of some delightful early nineteenth-century houses as well as a substantial row of Gothic dwellings complete with bay-windows (fig. 15). Opposite London Place is the sweep of the Park, rising up the hill to the trees. Morrell Avenue, lined by rather pleasant former Council houses of the inter-war period, has its attractions, while the warren of little streets between Morrell Avenue and the Cowley Road is as close-knit as any residential area in Oxford. Here small businesses, workshops, and stores mingle with houses, pubs, shops, halls, and churches. Garages, accommodation, specialist shops, and off-licences can all be found. This mixture makes the area interesting and contrasts with the tidy but boring housing estates elsewhere in Oxford.

St. Clement's has not yet deteriorated to the extent of St. Ebbe's despite the blighting effects of the threatened roadworks proposed by the infamous Meadow Road scheme. A new threat replaced the Meadow Road, however. The inner relief road was given the approval of the Secretary of State for the Environment and would have cut across from the west to a point at the very bottom of Headington Hill immediately opposite London Place. Quite apart from the appalling damage this road would have done to St. Margaret's Road and to north Oxford, south Oxford was bound to suffer, and so would large areas between the Abingdon Road and London Place. It is not just a matter of demolishing property to make way for the road, but a question of making life difficult for those whose houses adjoin the road but who are not bought out. A recent instance of this has been in Acklam Road in North Kensington, where the motorway passes only a few feet away from the bedroom windows, causing untold hardship. Even if the new road were shown stopping at the bottom of Headington Hill, does anyone seriously suppose that 'improvements' would not eventually have been carried out to Headington Hill and Marston Road, involving further environmental damage? The destruction of the fine trees, the raised footpath, the lovely Victorian cast-iron bridge, not to mention the damage to the lives and property of those who live in the vicinity, are high prices to pay for a road. Let us not forget roads are enormously expensive in purely constructional terms, but the *social* costs of anxiety, noise, damage to the quality of the city, and the deterioration of community life were never evaluated nor taken into account.

There were many people who believed that before such an expensive and irreversible step was taken, empirical experiments should have been made with traffic management, public transport systems, and the *prohibition* of the *private* motor-car in certain areas. If an experiment, lasting, say, two years, were made, using a really first-class integrated public transport system of buses, minicabs, taxis, minibuses, river buses, and so on, related to the railway and to out-of-town car parks, proved successful, then there would be no need to build an expensive road which cannot be demolished once it is built, nor can the destroyed houses and communities be reconstituted. St. Ebbe's is a case in point.

A few more years, and a few more blighting plans, could drive St. Clement's into the abyss of decay if the heavy hand of officialdom lies over it too long. There is a case for encouraging private investors, and especially owner-occupiers, to spend money on their property, freed from any threat. Both central fiscal policy and local planning policies

Fig. 11: *St. Clement's High Street, showing the small, essentially vertical emphasis of each individual unit.*

Below left: fig. 12 A pedestrian route beside the old Almshouses, leading from St. Clement's Street to Alma Place and Tyndale Road.

Below right: fig. 13 The pedestrian route leading to Tyndale Road

Top: fig. 14 The Almshouses in the background, showing potentially enhanceable areas in the foreground.

Bottom: fig. 15 London Place, showing the agreeable architectural character of this area.

Fig. 16: Gothic houses in London Place

would appear to be working against such a suggestion at present, however.

Fortunately, the Oxford Civic Society's pamphlet[1] was published in time, and in a subsequent Council election, the supporters of the road were outnumbered. Technically speaking, however, the blight of the road still remains until a new plan is approved.[2]

The unassuming qualities of St. Clement's as a whole should be appreciated now, before the area goes the way of so much else in Oxford. St. Clement's, like Jericho, Summertown, and other closely identifiable areas, is part and parcel of the structure of Oxford and its history[3].

[1] *Let's LIVE in Oxford,* Oxford Civic Society, 1969.
[2] In 1976, the road-scheme was again resurrected, and the battles may have to be fought all over again.
[3] 'The Erosion of Oxford II' by Adytum, *Oxford Mail,* 8 November 1968.

7
Jericho and the North

'Gradual renewal is a continuous
process of minor rebuilding and
renovation . . . responsive to social
and physical needs as they develop
and change.'

Department of the Environment
Circular 13/75

Fig. 1: The campanile of St. Barnabas rises above typical Jericho houses. This Italianate tower was built in 1872, and re-roofed in 1893.

The quotation under the chapter heading perhaps lacks the ancestry of some other pieces I have used to embellish other chapters. It is hardly deathless prose, but it marks a profoundly significant change in official attitudes.

Government circulars based on future renewal strategies[1] mark the end of official approval of comprehensive redevelopment. As from 1975, local authorities are advised to use gradual renewal, including renovation, so that the disruption of existing communities can be avoided.

Comprehensive clearance and redevelopment was a highly expensive and destructive solution. Communities were destroyed, social costs were not included, and many potentially fine buildings were wrecked because they lacked a bathroom, or because they needed repair because of years of bureaucratic blight. St. Ebbe's was a victim of the old methods.

It is a fact that the more eagerly authorities bought up huge areas of housing for demolition, the less likely housing was likely to go up to replace the destroyed property. Costs of new building put paid to such grandiose dreams, but more and more the energy consumption became a factor. Real capital, in the form of old buildings, was being squandered. The damage in national terms was colossal, and will probably never be put right now.

Gradual renewal and rehabilitation are attractive for their social benefits and financial advantages. Central government is only now recognising the need to control the rate of obsolescence, but in Oxford one area of the city was singled out in the 1960s for special treatment by the Planning Authority. The wholesale flattening of St. Ebbe's and the total inertia over the redevelopment had caused some worry. The threat of a local authority initiative in Jericho caused a tremendous 'resistance movement' among the inhabitants who, fortunately, had able leadership among those living in Jericho.

Gradual renewal rather than comprehensive redevelopment had an airing in various debates of a decade ago. Oxford City Council, however, anticipated later official policy as long ago as 1966 when a reasoned policy of continuous renewal was proposed for Jericho, a largely residential area lying to the west of Walton Street, between the railway and North Oxford. For the most part Jericho consists of two-storey mid-nineteenth-century terrace housing, with corner shops, pubs, and other buildings. It developed gradually from the time of William IV following the building of the University Press buildings in the area, and the growth of the railway and canalside activities. A foundry was established in Jericho that produced much of Oxford's cast-iron goods. A school by George Edmund Street, and the colossal Italianate Church of St. Barnabas by Sir Arthur Blomfield added style to the area (fig. 1). It is good to see that the parish the church serves is being rehabilitated. It is a pity that the quality of some of the designs could not be bettered, however, but surely it is encouraging that Jericho is not being battered into limbo as was the sad fate of St. Ebbe's. May St. Barnabas' church, designed more than a century ago, long stand over a renewed and better Jericho! It has perhaps one of the best Victorian church interiors in the whole area, and in Oxford is uniquely fine. Although unfinished, it is a glowingly resplendent interior, and outside, the functional and bold treatment of brick and

Fig. 2: A typical street scene in Jericho showing the traditional textured brickwork with yellow headers and red stretchers.

Fig. 3: A new development in the existing street. Buildings on the old building-line are much more successful than the examples shown in fig. 5.

rendering is a salutary lesson to those who have plastered their buildings with dozens of different materials in the hope, vain as it turns out, that something of quality will emerge.

Most of the streets in Jericho were built of numbers of short abutting terraces, usually by local builders, some of whose firms still survive in the area. Traditions of decorative brickwork survived in Jericho and fig. 2 shows a typical street scene.

Preliminary surveys showed houses of varying states of unfitness, with some well-maintained, but others were blighted by insecurity over which way the Council would jump. Some houses were in poor condition owing to lack of capital.

The results of the survey prompted some councillors to demand the complete razing of Jericho and its re-zoning for industry, but a social survey revealed a stable community, with most inhabitants keen to stay. Gradual renewal was decided upon, and private owners were encouraged to improve their properties. Grants were made available, and purchase of houses by agreement rather than by compulsion was used where it was necessary for the Council to take over property. A number of houses thus passed into Council ownership, and this ensured a wide social mix.

Many 'improvements', however, such as fake shutters, are totally out of character, and could be considered to detract from the simple architectural elements. Private enterprise has been hard at work slotting new buildings within the fabric, in some cases successfully maintaining the scale (fig. 3), but unfortunately the Planning Department's love for dull brown bricks has prevailed. When a lively tradition of using strongly coloured bricks existed in much of the surviving fabric in the area of Jericho and Walton Street (fig. 4) it is hard to understand why a dull, lifeless, boring brick should have been insisted

Fig. 4: The buildings in Walton Street with their lively tradition of strongly coloured bricks.

Right: fig. 5 New buildings set back in Jericho. Note the useless ill-kempt grass, and the fact that the set-back destroys the scale and enclosure of the street. The relationship between the solids and the voids in the new building is weak and unresolved.

Left: fig. 6 New flats in Jericho with the foundry in the background. If a policy of partial clearance, much rehabilitation, and a combination of private and public endeavour had prevailed in St. Ebbe's, much hardship would have been avoided.

upon. Elsewhere in Jericho, new developments have not quite lived up to the old developments (fig. 5). The restless lines of the buildings on the left pay little heed to the traditional terrace pattern, while the squalid little patches of grass on the right, fenced in with the Good Taste metal rail, will not only be difficult to maintain, but help to erode the very qualities that give Jericho a character that people want to enjoy.

Renewal in Jericho is infinitely preferable to the disaster of St. Ebbe's, even though quite large chunks of Jericho have been razed, with most unfortunate visual, and, one suspects, social results. The plan has, to some extent, retained an existing stable community, as well as saved a number of small businesses that provide work and services. New elements have been slotted in, and private enterprise has combined with the local authority in a constructive manner. The foundry has built a block of pleasant flats adjacent to the works (fig. 6) with a car park in the basement. The foursquare 'panelled' style of the building is very much of the last 1950s and early 1960s, although the building was only completed in the early 1970s. There is so much evidence of simple windows on brick walls in the Jericho area that it is perhaps a pity that the vernacular tradition was not carried through in this large and important building by the foundry gates. If the windows had been treated as holes in the walls, part of the 'panelled' effect would have been removed, and the building would have related more to its surroundings.

The rejection of a 'comprehensive redevelopment' approach has prevented wholesale blighting as well as a great reduction in the

Left: fig. 7 An ugly modern lamp with two signs. A lantern of more sympathetic design could have been mounted directly on the wall, as could the signs. The pole is quite unnecessary, is a waste of money and is extremely ugly.

Right: fig. 8 Beautiful old brickwork and a fine old lamp on a bracket of pleasing design. The new lamp-post is not needed. The lantern could be mounted under the eaves. This picture shows erosion in progress.

numbers of houses. The declaration of Jericho as a General Improvement Area would considerably help matters.

There are, however, several points that need to be considered in relation to the physical changes of the area. In many instances, façades have been unbalanced by the insertion of inappropriate windows and doors. New blocks, replacing property at the end of its life, do not always respect the existing fabric. In some cases, set-backs, different patterns of fenestration, and other factors spoil the flow and scale of streets.

Many areas of North Oxford, consisting of the poorer type of property, have undergone recent changes. Set-backs and changing scale are apparent (see fig. 5). Street lights and signs almost kill the architecture. There are many instances where lanterns could have been mounted directly on the walls, and so could the road signs. It is a complete mystery to me why the pole was used at all in the example in fig. 7. Fig. 8 provides an even greater conundrum. Here, a new standard has just been erected adjacent to a traditional wall-mounted lantern on a pleasing bracket. The traditional design grows out of the corner of the agreeable little two-storey house. The new pole is actually touching the wall! This means wasted metal, more ugliness, and a retreat from the recommendations of the Code of

Fig. 9: The walled and enclosed character removed in Summertown.

Fig. 10: Recently, a charming railing existed here. It has been replaced by this dwarf wall.

Practice C.P. 1004 that recommends wall-mounted fittings in such cases. The lantern could have been fixed unobtrusively at eaves level.

In Jericho, some developments have fully taken into account the possibilities of walls for enclosure. In Summertown, however, walls are coming down by 'the yard', and many buildings have vanished. The corner of Rogers Street and Middle Way is now a car park. There is no attempt to screen this, but a silly little wall about a foot high defines the bounds (fig. 9). There was an elegant iron railing about four feet high on the line of the dwarf wall shown in fig. 10. It bounded a graveyard. It is a great pity the old railing could not have been retained, adapted, and repainted. The dwarf wall does nothing for enclosure or the townscape.

The gradual changes to the shopping areas of Summertown over the years have added up to an almost total transformation. The east side has had its scale utterly altered. The old Dewdrop has been dwarfed by development, while the traffic-generating power of Summertown will be apparent to all.

It is this piecemeal erosion that is particularly worrying in North Oxford as a whole. Here, in a landscape of mature trees, at their best in May (fig. 11), great Victorian and Edwardian villas rise up in substantial grounds. The influence of John Claudius Loudon, that irritating but phenomenally prolific Scot, is everywhere apparent in the juxtaposition of colours and sizes of trees and other plants. Hideous modern street-lighting and road-signs painted on the surfaces of the carriageways

Fig. 11: The landscape of mature trees in North Oxford that needs careful conservation now.

Fig. 12: Stone-fronted crescent in Park Town

Fig. 13: Park Terrace showing the arch

Fig. 14: A villa in Park Town

do not help visual quality. It is significant that Oxford's first Conservation Area was in North Oxford. It embraced Park Town; part of the
Banbury Road between Park Town and North Parade Avenue; parts of
Canterbury, Winchester, Norham, Bradmore, and Crick Roads; North
Parade Avenue; Norham Gardens; Church Walk; and the Church of SS.
Philip and James, Woodstock Road. It was not an adventurous Conservation Area, and although it contained some of the first Victorian houses
in Oxford, it left an immense amount out. Since designation, the area
outside the Conservation Area has been subjected to increasing pressures
for change.

   Park Town was laid out between 1853 and 1855. The original plan
was for elegant villas and terraces, with 'ornamental gardens and pleasant
grounds well stocked with trees and flowering shrubs'. It is formed of
two stone-fronted crescents north and south of an elliptical central
garden (fig. 12); a brick-and-stucco crescent divided by an archway at the
east end called Park Terrace (fig. 13); and large Italianate villas with
enormous bracketed eaves and one or two later villas (fig. 14). The
architect of Park Town was Samuel Lipscomb Seckham. His work was
probably influenced by J. B. Papworth's development at Cheltenham,
and by other speculative housing schemes in London where villas and
terraces are found together.

   Park Town, however, is atypical. The standard North Oxford
domestic building is of grey or red brick with stone dressings, distinctly
Gothic in flavour, and plenty of fine examples survive (see fig. 18). The
designers were William Wilkinson, Charles Buckeridge, Frederic Codd,
John Gibbs, and others. Nearly all the North Oxford houses of the 1860s,
1870s, and 1880s are large, gabled, and vaguely Gothic in style. The

Fig. 15: A new horizontal building at the west junction of St. Margaret's Road and Woodstock Road.

Fig. 16: A new horizontal building at the east junction of St. Margaret's Road and Woodstock Road

whole effect is sober, slightly severe, even earnest, set in luxurious planting.

In the 1970s, great changes have been taking place as demand for land increases and the big villas get further subdivided. Several buildings have been erected which do not respect the intricate, gabled forms found in North Oxford, and several crucial sites have been redeveloped

160

Fig. 17: The entrance to North Parade Avenue. Note the Papworthian villa on the right.

recently with buildings of *horizontal* emphasis (figs. 15, 16). All the traditional buildings of Gothic North Oxford are *vertical*. Even classical Park Town is vertical in its essential features.

North Parade Avenue must be one of the most interesting little streets in Oxford: with its pubs, shops, and houses it represents an ideal mixture for social activity, and is very much the centrepiece of a delightful area. The entrance to North Parade Avenue on the Banbury Road is flanked by simple buildings partially converted for commercial use on the south side, but with two very fine villas on the north side, very much in the manner of Papworth at Cheltenham (fig. 17). Immediately to the north, however, are two fine Gothic houses (fig. 18). The great church of SS. Philip and James, by Street, stands on Woodstock Road, and provides an architectural focus (see chap. 4, fig. 15).

Costs of repairs, heating, and demand for a higher density of land use are putting great pressures on North Oxford. Comprehensive conservation policies for the area as a whole lagged behind the early erosion. Many houses are let out on a room basis, and many are sub-divided. As a result, much of the fabric needs urgent repair, while many of the grounds are ill-kempt and overgrown. Overall policies should have anticipated demand for change at the time the first (very small) Conservation Area was designated in 1968. In only a few years the damage to North Oxford has been considerable.

[1]*Housing Act 1974: Renewal Strategies.* D.O.E. Circular No. 13/75. and *Housing Act 1974: Housing Action Areas, Priority Neighbourhoods, and General Improvement Areas.* D.O.E. Circular No. 14/75.

Fig. 18: Two Gothic villas on the Banbury Road

3

The Blighted Suburbs

'. . . and, gentlemen, what a *whole*
Oxford is!'

Sir John Coleridge:
G. W. E. Russell *Collections and
Recollections*

The probable revision of his remarks by Sir John Coleridge, had he had the opportunity of seeing Oxford today, is a subject not unfit for speculation. Omission of the 'w' would better describe some parts of the fabric, and certainly Oxford is no longer a visual or cohesive entity. It straggles, it sprawls, it has lost its *form*.

In previous chapters I drew attention to certain objects and places of quality which add something of charm to the environment. I also pointed out how some items, small in themselves, can destroy a visual excellence which might have survived. In this chapter, I shall select a few examples of places which lack anything of beauty, but are instead areas of unmitigated ugliness and banality.

Rose Hill, perhaps the most potentially beautiful site in Oxford, has been ruined. You would imagine that the view over the City, where 'the eye travels down to Oxford's towers', would have been exploited, and benefits drawn from it. You would also think that the qualities of adjacent Iffley, which lies lower down the slopes on the bank of the river, might have impinged on the designers of Rose Hill. These hopes, however, turn out to be without foundation. Instead, the estate is as amorphous as possible, and the view over Oxford clearly does not exist, for the layout ignores it.

The development is centred on a windswept space of semi-bald earth (fig. 1) which is surrounded by a series of unrelated buildings and a collection of the most incredibly hideous lamp-posts. Both Barton and Rose Hill have quotas of prefabricated houses, broken down fencing, and the ubiquitous lamp-posts all calculated to combine to form a visual

Fig. 1: The centre of Rose Hill, bald and windswept

Fig. 2: Cherry trees and ugly fencing do little to help the visual squalor

desert of the worst kind which a few cherry trees do little to improve (fig. 2). Even where brick has been used to construct the houses, the design can hardly be called inspired, while the post and wire fencing, useless little strips of grass, and horrible lamps do little to enhance the visual qualities of the area. Naturally, the post-War period, with its stringent controls, was not a time of great plenty, but recent ministerial panaceas, such as a return to the pre-fab, should fill us with horror and foreboding. We have not *all* forgotten the suffocating grip of austerity, the frustrations of governmental control, and the sheer visual ugliness that resulted.

Fig. 3: Scruffiness

The slopes of Shotover Hill are beautiful. Unfortunately, they are subject to very dense use for recreation, and this excessive use could well destroy the qualities which it has. As the ground slopes gently down over what once must have been lovely meadows, aspects of modern civilisation blighted the area in recent times (fig. 3). There is no doubt

165

Left: fig. 4 The architectural and town-scape lessons of Turl Street

Facing page: fig. 5 The centre of Blackbird Leys, consisting of a number of buildings cleverly unrelated to one another.

that poles, wires, 'temporary' housing, caravans and the like, are visually ruinous, while attempts to solve the housing problem on the cheap create dilemmas all along the line.

It seems almost incredible that a city with the architectural lessons of Oxford should have such dreary suburbs. Focus, enclosure, nature, aesthetic quality, and homogeneity are all apparent in Turl Street (fig. 4). The examples cited lack all these qualities except the homogeneity of generalised ugliness. Compare the traditional lamp-brackets in chapter four with the dreariness of the lamps, roads and houses in figs. 1 and 2 and perhaps the message will strike answering chords in those citizens of Oxford who are genuinely worried about the destruction of their city and the desecration of their own environment.

We have today legislation and power to control our surroundings in ways impossible to older generations. It is possible we are misusing those powers, or perhaps it is because we just have not got the will or the taste to make the best use of them.

My purpose in showing this selection of pictures and writing these comments is to stimulate comment and perhaps greater concern among my fellow-citizens for what is happening to Oxford. Public demand can change things and it is my hope that those who care for the look of their surroundings may feel moved to ask for improvements in standards generally to help to clear up the shoddiness of much of Oxford. The private individual can do much to help.

I shall now venture out to the far suburbs of Cowley to offer some comments on this area. It is a curious fact that Oxford, so long split by

Town and Gown considerations, seems to have had its dual character
expressed most forcibly by its two settlements — Oxford and Cowley.
The natural break seems to be at Magdalen Bridge, and east of there a
different town exists, far removed from the spirit of Oxford. One town
is old, mellow and beautiful, while the other is new, brash, ugly and
already rather tired looking.

The care, the money, the creativity and the sensibility that made
Oxford could have made a beautiful Cowley, industry and all. There is
no reason why industry should not be expressed in beauty and in
dignity. The people who work in such an industry should be housed in
a decent environment, with all the things that could enrich their lives,
and in turn, the lives of all the citizens of Oxford.

In Blackbird Leys we have a major planned housing estate in
Oxford with supposedly all amenities. Let us look at what is actually
there.

The centre of Blackbird Leys is composed of a series of totally
unrelated buildings housing different functions grouped around a
miserable piece of ground which is, in fact, nothing more than a roundabout. The group of buildings includes a pub, a health centre, a
community centre, a church, a library, shops, a public lavatory and a
tower block of flats. Look at the Community Centre (fig. 5) seen from
the 'open space' — a hamfisted design near a scruffy bit of land not
improved by telegraph poles and apologetic planting. The church is an
interesting design on its own but it was clearly impossible to relate it to
the surrounding hotch-potch. The library is a very decent little design,
the main criticisms being that again it does not relate, and

Fig. 6: The lumpish and inelegant flats at Blackbird Leys

that the large areas of painted wood will need a great deal of maintenance to keep the building in a reasonable state.

Turning full circle we see the shopping centre, a mediocre design
with far too many materials used when half as many would have done,
and then the dominant of the space, the tower block of flats. Viewed
from across the space it presents an unedifying sight (fig. 6). Lumpish
and inelegant, it sits a dead weight on the land. Its red and yellow
panels and its very form betray a lack of sensitivity in design, while this
very philosophy of providing tall blocks of flats is now totally dis-
credited. In the picture, the quality of treatment being given to the
open spaces is clearly seen.

Fig. 7: Another inelegant block. Note the brick panel, and the unresolved relationships between solids and voids.

Fig. 8: An unexciting local shopping centre

Below: fig. 9 Boring subtopia, only enlivened by the distant Cowley Centre.

Left: fig. 10 The overall architecture is a curious hotch-potch with clumsy junctions, huge areas of glass, and coloured panelling.

Further travel about the estate can be depressing. A view through some of the most recent development, which should represent the most up-to-date features of design, reveals a dreariness it is sad to see. One of the newest buildings on the estate lacks all grace and sensitivity, with fenestration devoid of serenity. Note the relatively meaningless panel of brickwork, the mean entrance and the poor proportions of the relationship between windows and voids (fig. 7).

Neighbourhood shopping centres are unexciting, as is clearly demonstrated in fig. 8. The road from Blackbird Leys towards Cowley Centre leads us past featureless landscape with monotonous housing. As the eye travels right the dominants are cars, roads, useless little grass verges, and singularly ugly housing. Can any citizen of Oxford sincerely defend the dullness or the boredom shown in fig. 9, admittedly relieved somewhat by the appearance of Cowley Centre at the end of the road?

Nearer Cowley Centre we spot the same design of dwelling used at the Headington Roundabout. Elsewhere on the estate, many groups of buildings have a plethora of materials. The large areas of paintwork require regular maintenance that is clearly already far too much for the departments concerned.

Cowley Centre itself is very much a product of the brash late nineteen-fifties and early nineteen-sixties. The tower block over a walkway, together with the square and avenues, created almost perfect wind-tunnel effects. The overall architectural statement is a curious hotch-potch, with clumsy junctions, huge areas of glass, and coloured panelling (fig. 10). There are few edifying things about the journey you make into this man-made, planned, subsidised wilderness. Some will say there are worse areas elsewhere, and I would agree with this,

170

but it would be difficult to argue that *any* of it is good enough, not only in human terms, but in the context of Oxford.

People who live in an industrial area deserve as good treatment as anyone else. The whole Cowley area should be looked upon as the main industrial part of Oxford, so badly handled, so messily planned, so piece-meal developed, that it represents a major *erosion* of part of Oxford's heritage.

It is not within the scope of this book to discuss the economic viability of having a motor industry here, but to draw attention to an area which presented a challenge to designers to solve a difficult problem. This has manifestly been unresolved, and the result is there for you and myself to judge, as judge we must if we are to do our civic duty. It is up to us to criticise, to agitate, to demand better standards. Let us ask now for thousands of trees to be planted in Blackbird Leys, and I mean trees — not little miniatures, but beeches, pines, chestnuts, oaks, planes, limes, birches and all the variety that gives North Oxford its wonderful qualities. Planting could save it, and the City could encourage individual families to plant trees themselves, while children could be advised through schools and youth workers each to plant a tree for the future. If this community sense of involvement and pride in the environment were to be fostered, the trees would survive and vandalism would very likely decline. But it needs thousands of trees, not just the few the local authority can plant.

The suggestion could be given a try. European Architectural Heritage Year 1975 should have offered the stimulus for such an effort.

Let us now turn our attention to some of the other unfortunate developments that have taken place in the suburbs of Oxford. Imagine that you are a tourist and that you are approaching Oxford by the A40 for the first time. You have long heard about the 'dreaming spires', and you arrive on the outskirts of Oxford with high excitement. They are, I submit, squalid and dreary, and not good enough for Oxford. The surroundings do not help either, and the usual plethora of signs, lamp-posts, municipal planting (in the most genteel fashion), roads and barrenness contribute visual deadliness.

Near by, on the way down to Barton Estate, we have the by now familiar sight of signs, horrible lamp-posts, indifferent housing and a lay-out which, to say the least, is uninspired. This is Oxford, and the standards we are getting are not up to the priceless heritage of the past (fig. 11).

Near the Northern By-pass lies North Way Estate. It should by now be apparent that the so-called 'Estate' is no answer to the housing problem. It is cheaper to raise housing standards by adapting existing stock than to build anew. We spend only about a quarter of what we should spend on maintenance and only a fraction of what we should be pouring into rehabilitation. This means there must be waste, and so existing housing decays too quickly, because of official policy. Housing suffers from discrimination, and is subject to tax in the form of rates. Too much is spent on subsidised rents, and social pressures prevent the charging of reasonable rents. The result is that the environment gets run down, and buildings cannot be maintained. The policy of providing large 'Estates' means that there is no individual pride in ownership and little incentive to look after and improve property. Apart from these

Fig. 11: An uninspired scene

Fig. 12: Dullness personified in a shopping centre

aspects, public 'Estates' tend to be poorly designed and also tend to accentuate class problems. Where people should be meeting and living in large groups of multi-class background, the council 'Estate' tends to encourage one-class areas much more than was the case in the last century. There are also problems with age-groups, and a fully balanced mix is difficult to achieve.

The centrepiece of such an area is all too often the sort of thing shown in fig. 12. There is little of merit or inspiration in the design of the 'shopping centre' shown in the photograph, and it is really too bad that Oxford is getting, and has got, such buildings at all. Frequently the mistake is made of assuming that a visually boring area can be redeemed by a 'vertical feature'. Such a 'vertical feature' all too often turns out to be a package-deal block of flats. Such a solution must be arrived at with no regard to the scale of the countryside, the scale of the area, and the scale of *human beings*. It would be interesting if the people who have advocated blocks of flats could demonstrate that they have an eye for scale and that they are aware of the social consequences caused by such developments and the political and fiscal decisions taken to promote them. Tall blocks of flats are poor solutions to the housing problem, and it must be remembered that they work out enormously expensive to construct without saving land. Nobody appears to have taken into account social costs, costs of future demolition, or the difficulties of power failures. Apart from anything else, it can scarcely be admitted by *anyone* that the block of flats shown in fig. 6 represents good design.

A medal for bad Civic Design should go to the scene in fig. 13. There is no doubt here that the dominant feature is the road. Look at the hideous lamps and other crude details. This is downright thoughtlessness. The space could be most pleasant if avenues of trees were planted to effectively reduce the width of the street.

The Barton—Rose Hill image is presented by figs. 1 and 2. Observe the crudities of the housing design; the dreadful poles and lamps; the broken down fencing; the road and pavements. Such planting as exists is almost pathetic. Again, one looks in vain for evidence that the lessons of beautiful Oxford have been learned at any level.

The beautiful little pub in St. Ebbe's (fig. 14) sits alone and amputated from its surroundings. Here the road-builders have created a framework within which it will be difficult, if not almost impossible, to create anything worthwhile as an area of visual quality. There is little indication that the area has been planned; rather the roads appear to have been arbitrarily placed, with no over-all plan for the area. Clearly this must be the case, as the road system has little resemblance to the plan shown in the Development Plan Review. It is a matter for speculation to consider how long it will be before the last old buildings in St. Ebbe's are swept away by roadworks. The approach to St. Ebbe's, which was the subject of another chapter, reflects the standards that have been applied to the suburbs.

There needs to be great care taken where Headington and the Quarry are concerned. Both places are still fortunately relatively unspoiled but much damage could be done by ill-advised road-widening and by ungracious 'infill'. This latter euphemism really means a process which never stops, and which can destroy the visual qualities of a village just as effectively as an over-zealous road engineer or a bulldozer.

Both Headington Village and the Quarry are essentially villages which have been absorbed by an Oxford as it exploded because of the invention of the motor-car.

Fig. 15 shows a delightful old building in Headington which, together with the buildings on the left, forms an excellent 'stop' to the end of the street leading from the traffic lights on the London Road. Fig. 16 demonstrates how effective the group on the left of the first building actually is when viewed from some distance away. Note the foil provided by the tree on the right, and imagine how poorer the scene would be without it. There is nothing spectacular here; only decent unpretentious architecture, worthy of the attentions of preservation groups, but vulnerable nevertheless, and extremely valu-

able, especially since so much erosion has already taken place in Oxford.

   By the church, the street is full of good buildings in the local tradition (fig. 17) and part of our heritage which we should endeavour to keep. In most cases properties like this can be brought up to date with minor expenditure, and, although these particular buildings all

Fig. 13: Oxford suburbia, dominated by the road, and fringed by hideous lamps.

Fig. 14: A charming, classical little pub in St. Ebbe's 'sits alone, amputated from its surroundings'.

Fig. 15: A house in Old Headington, providing an excellent visual 'stop'.

Left: fig. 16 Old Headington. The tree frames the building at the end.

Below: fig. 17 Good buildings in the vernacular tradition at Old Headington

seem in good condition, many others exist in and near Oxford which, with some investment, could be rescued.

The Quarry possesses some excellent things. Fig. 18 shows the Chequers pub with its magnificent tree casting a shadow on the warm stone walls, and I can only ask again why more trees are not being planted in crucial positions like this.

The village is full of an interesting series of footpaths which interconnect and weave through the matrix of the settlement. The paths usually are bounded by fine stone walls with plants trailing down over the tops, such as the path shown in fig. 19.

Fig. 20 shows clearly the varied topography of the site of the village, and it is an agreeable inter-relation of forms which typifies the subtle quality of the development. The porch on the house on the right is a little unfortunate, for the house is a very decent design, while the blank space on the left of the picture badly needs a large tree.

Fig. 21 shows how perfectly ordinary housing groups, undistinguished in themselves, are made tremendously exciting and even delightful by the careful and intelligent preservation of good trees which give foci and foils to otherwise commonplace scenes.

In the Quarry nature, fortunately, has not been crushed out nor reduced to the pitiable level of cherry-tree and grass-verge suburbia, which is not really nature at all, but some dreadful parody where nothing can actually grow without being weeded out, pruned, cut down or subjected to the prophylactic activities of those who must regulate, control and prevent natural growth, until it looks as though nothing is growing at all.

Let us have more trees, more walls, more *real* nature in our suburbs, and not masses of concrete, tarmac, little boxes unrelated to their site, and all the other horrors of the contemporary scene. There can be little doubt that the average suburban landscape in its worst form sums up the condition of modern suburban man, alienated as

Below: fig. 18 The Chequers Pub at Headington Quarry, with its splendid tree

Left: fig. 19 The Quarry's many good points include a series of footpaths like this.

Below: fig. 20 The interesting topography of the Quarry is varied. The addition of a tree such as may be seen in fig. 18 would be beneficial.

Left: fig. 21 Trees and walls make quite ordinary groups of buildings interesting and delightful.

he is from the *major* problems of existence.

Society leaves the individual only trivial decisions to make. Man, the employee, buying his house on borrowed money or paying a subsidised council rent, is far from the appreciation of hard property and from the sense of responsibility going with it. Suburbia, divorced from nature, without the grandeur of mighty trees to remind its inhabitants how insignificant they really are; without the true integration of buildings and nature; without the cultural, social and economic possibilities of rational *urban* life, is the *symbol* and habitat of modern man. His participation in affairs is now safely relegated to watching television, as far from the true realities of his environment as he is from the things that really matter.

Headington Village and the Quarry fortunately possess something better, and I hope I have given some indication as to what that is.

9

Oxford in its Setting

'I have never seen Oxford since,
excepting its spires, as they are seen
from the railway.'

John Henry, Cardinal Newman:
*History of My Religious Opinions
from 1841 to 1845*

Fig. 1: The ring road presents a landscape of incredibly harsh ugliness

The approaches to Oxford all lead to the corset that surrounds the city. This corset rings the whole of Oxford. It is a sobering experience to travel round this ring road to see just what the twentieth century and one of its most devastating products, the mass-produced motor-car, have done to the formerly pleasant country round Oxford and its satellites and suburbs.

Near the factories, at Cowley, the ring road presents a landscape of incredibly harsh ugliness. Apart from the expanse of road surface, the signs, serried rows of monstrous lamps, and grey, soulless housing, all add up to a picture of depressed and depressing environment (fig. 1).

Near by, between the Works and Headington, is a landscape from the world of concentration camps and inhumanity. The fact that the gentle, charming surroundings of a national treasure should be mal-treated in this way is nothing short of a disgrace, not only locally, but nationally.

Squalor and decrepitude are not confined to Cowley. Between the Summertown roundabout and that of Headington lies typical litter of our age. Dual carriageways are the logical extension of road-building, when roads create a demand for more road space. The examination of the ditches and hedgerows adjacent to the ring road reveals an assort-ment of junk of all sorts: bits of machinery, sundry objects, and even

Fig. 2: The dual carriageway, an expensive carpet for motor-cars, passes by grey, dreary houses.

Fig. 3: A wasteland of broken fencing

abandoned cars or pieces of cars. When a mechanised society cannot even dispose of its unwanted cast-offs in a manner which does not damage natural features or the visual qualities of the environment, the measure of that society's civilisation is in question. Society does not stop at motor-car ownership. Having destroyed cities, towns, and villages, as well as large tracts of countryside by providing for these destructive objects, it then litters the land with cars and bits of cars when they outlive their allotted time. All the metal cans, cast-off seats, doors, and other bits and pieces are thrown into hedgerows, fields, lakes, streams and ponds. I recently saw a stretch of water near the northern end of the western by-pass which had received more than its fair share of the junk left by a philistine and destructive public. Pollution is an international problem. Conservation Year has come and gone, yet pollution and litter continue to spread. A society that believes that food comes from supermarkets rather than from the earth knows nothing of ecological factors. Nature is being maltreated. Mankind will eventually pay for such thoughtlessness and wasteful attitudes.

The crudities of the present age are summed up in the dismal comment on our failure to plan attractive homes and civilised surroundings *within a landscape of once incomparable charm and beauty*. The dual carriageway, an expensive carpet for motor-cars, passes by grey, dreary houses (fig. 2). There is hardly any reminder of nature within many of these developments, although the hill of Shotover rises above the landscape. Shotover faces some man-made ugliness, and it is all the more depressing to compare natural beauty with what our own century has done to Oxford's setting.

The sides of the by-passes are wastelands of broken fencing (fig. 3), mud, puddles, and general squalor and pollution. Litter, tyre tracks, signs, and a windy limbo from which humanity has fled except to deposit rubbish, all add up to an indictment and a warning. It is perhaps worth asking ourselves if this is the landscape, the distressed England, that we want for our descendants and for ourselves, or if we do not care any more (fig. 4).

Other monuments to our age are seen from the ring road. No longer do the old churches of the Hinkseys to the west offer us those amiable foci at the ends of paths from the city. Instead, the colloquially named 'Botley Cathedral' dominates the western approaches. This building does not celebrate Christianity, however, but is a proudly assertive temple to the motor-car (fig. 5). It is impossible to look at Oxford from Cumnor now without being aware of this somewhat inelegant addition. The distant towers and spires which Matthew Arnold loved to view from Cumnor Hill are dwarfed by this grandiose building in the foreground. It is no longer true that the

> . . . air-swept lindens yield
> Their scent, and rustle down their perfumed showers
> Of bloom on the bent grass where I am laid,
> And bower me from the August sun with shade;
> And the eye travels down to Oxford's towers.

Instead the eye is distracted by pylons and by 'Botley Cathedral'. The 'Scholar Gypsy' would have good reason for coming

> to Oxford and his friends no more.

Despite all the lip-service paid to planning, and all the expensive machinery we pay for to ensure proper land-use and the control of amenity, it is clear that ugliness, waste, squalor, expediency, and a disregard for those priceless immeasurable aspects of our heritage are all on the increase. The wanton savaging of the legacy of our forefathers is rampant.

Striding across the countryside and up the slopes of that delightful

range of hills where Cumnor and Wytham nestle, are the other giant
destroyers of the gentle rural landscape (fig. 6). Pylons, pylons, and yet
more pylons disfigured, injured and blotted a wonderful landscape, an
essential part of Oxford's setting. They march up hills and down the
other side. They stride across the countryside. We no longer have a
landscape. The twentieth century has thought it better to give us wirescape.

Since the War, many examples of visual squalor have been provided.
A photographic record of some horrors taken over the last seven years
tells its own tale. At Headington, there are plenty of patches of derelict
and mutilated land. Posts, signs, boxes and ill-kempt land contribute to
the visual anarchy.

*Fig. 4: Is this the landscape, the
distressed England, that we want for our
descendants?*

Fig. 5: 'Botley Cathedral'

Fig. 6: Striding across the countryside are the giant destroyers of the gentle, rural landscape.

    Wirescape is not confined to pylons. On the by-pass near South Hinksey, further examples can be found. It is not a question of just wires and poles, but of all sorts of vertical clutter and bad design that makes the visual scene an aesthetic slum. Hurtfully ugly lamps and standards stagger down the road, while telegraph poles, signs, muddy and untidy verges, and all the paraphernalia of the suburban highway abound (fig. 7).

    Roundabouts are among the chief offenders. It is the jungle of

lamps, the resultant glare, and the proliferation of signs (fig. 8) that, apart from the noise, appearance, and smell of traffic, contribute to the disorder of these intersections. Bollards which can be illuminated, bright shiny signs, lamp posts, directives, balding grass verges, painted signs on the road surfaces themselves, all add up to confusion.

The ring road is often the first impression of a city that a traveller gets. On a misty day, he will see nothing of the celebrated skyline of Oxford. Even on a clear day, there are only a few places where that skyline may be seen. It will be the squalor of broken fencing, the mud, the litter, and the ugliness that the traveller will be aware of first.

Those who have travelled over the old Autobahn from Ostend to the south will remember the breathtaking view of Limburg Cathedral as it rises up from the River Lahn. Oxford's skyline is much less dramatic, much more English. Somehow, to me at any rate, the most nostalgic and lovely view of Oxford is that to be seen over the yellow-flowered fields of Port Meadow from the Godstow and Wolvercote direction.

A more distant view from the by-pass, when the sun is shining down on the golden warm stone of the old city, could have been wonderful. Pylons and all the other disruptive elements that have appeared in recent years have spoiled the potential and the memory.

Facing page: fig. 7 Gibbets on the by-pass

Below: fig. 8 The proliferation of signs and other objects

Hard surfaces for cars; ugly buildings; wirescape; and other visual intrusions sum up the current situation. It is not just Oxford and its suburbs that are suffering, but the setting as well. The Erosion of Oxford is widespread and catching. The damage is colossal.

If the hills around Oxford are important, so also are the historic settlements that nestle in their shelter. One of the finest of all such villages is Wytham. In 1943 a record was issued by the Oxford Preservation Trust on the acquisition of Wytham Abbey and Estate by the University of Oxford. In that record it was stated that 'the happy combination . . . of benefaction and purchase by which the University has . . . acquired the Wytham Estate constitutes an historic event of outstanding importance. By this transaction there pass under the aegis of the University more than 3,000 acres of land incomparably situated, on the western confines of the city of Oxford . . .'[1] The record continued by saying that the passing of this estate 'into the care of the University is an event . . . which means much to the citizens of Oxford; for it ensures that the unspoilt village of Wytham and its attendant woodlands and water-meadows will never fall a prey to speculative development'.[2]

The last private owner of the estate, Mr. Raymond W. ffennell, was well known for his concern about the hills around Oxford. He entered into a Deed of Agreement with the University in 1942 in which he expressed the need to preserve the natural beauties of the estate, and he, as Grantor, declared his willingness to leave the guardianship of the woodlands in the 'kindly sympathy' of the University.[3] There was also provision in the Deed for continuing services to the young, especially in the form of out-of-door schools. The price was fixed at far less than the valuation so that 'no dwelling houses should ever be erected on the Follies and Seacourt Meadows' and that the University should 'act generously . . . giving special facilities that will tend to the happiness and welfare of children and young persons . . .'.[4]

Mr. ffennell was anxious that the estate should not be regarded as an 'asset to be developed so as to yield a good income return but preserved in a large measure as an adjunct to the valuable gardens and open spaces of Oxford . . .'[5] It is absolutely clear from the Deed that Mr. ffennell granted the estate on condition that its natural beauty should be preserved for all time. He entrusted the University with this in mind. Parts of the estate were to be totally exempt from any possibility of being built on. These parts were Wytham village and its immediate vicinity, Wytham Great Wood, Marley Wood Plantation, and the Seacourt Meadows. Outside these areas some building would be permitted 'for additional research, educational and recreational purposes'.[6]

Since Mr. ffennell's great and generous gesture, more than thirty years have passed. In 1969 it was interesting to examine just how far the University and the Preservation Trust appeared to have changed in attitudes, perhaps not intentionally, nevertheless that was the impression given by events at the time. *Utque solebamus consumere longa loquendo Tempora, sermonem deficiente die.* Perhaps also because *tempora mutantur, et nos mutamur in illis.*

Wytham is remarkable. It is so because it is beautiful. It is still relatively unspoiled and it stands in country that is surprisingly rural, well-wooded, and hilly. It is four miles west of Oxford, and access to

Fig. 9: The approach to Wytham from the by-pass

it is from the by-pass or through Wolvercote (fig. 9). It is amazing it
has survived in its present form until now. Everywhere around Oxford
are villages which have been ruined. Wytham is therefore unique, not
only because of its exquisite charm, but because it is the last surviving
village that Oxford not overwhelmed by 'infill', 'development', 'redevelopment', or 'expansion'. So far, therefore, the University has
honoured the terms on which it obtained the property.

In 1969, however, it seemed to many environmentalists that a
change of policy was being formulated. A report was prepared for the
Oxford University Chest entitled *Wytham: How to save the village,* and
this proposed a certain amount of development. The report was accom-
panied by a statement by the University Chest Committee in which it
was made plain that new housing was proposed. The reason for these
proposals were based upon arguments that at first appeared to be
reasonable. It was stated in the report that several cottages were empty,
that the school was closing, and that the village was dying. Empty
houses quickly deteriorate. In an area where housing demand is very
great (the Oxford region saw huge expansion of population in the
1960s) these cottages would have been occupied long ago had it been
permitted. Clearly, the decision not to let them was a conscious one,
and was probably influenced by the desire to wait until the report had
been prepared before any far-reaching decisions were taken.

The report was well-intentioned, and contained an admirable
analysis of the qualities of the village. Unfortunately, its proposals
could have been the beginning of the end for Wytham.

189

Left: fig. 10 Part of the Linch Farm outbuildings, before conversion, showing how important the building is at a key site in the village.

Right: fig. 11 Wytham's gentle and unobtrusive qualities depend on its walls, trees and the simple dignity of a vernacular architecture.

Many cottages were tied to farms, and agricultural practice has changed, and is changing beyond all recognition. Wytham is no longer a rural community. In an open market, the charms of Wytham, combined with its proximity to Oxford, would have ensured that all the empty buildings would have been in use in the 1960s. Linch Farm, in the centre of the village, was no longer used because large farms had replaced the old units. The cottages of the farm and its outbuildings, which the report rightly pointed out as being of great importance visually in the fabric of Wytham, could have been converted for housing or other purposes long before the work was actually carried out (fig. 10).

It is absolutely essential that the existing fabric of Wytham should be restored and adapted. The landscape and walled character must be conserved (fig. 11). Whatever happens, no infill and no major development of the nature indicated by the report should ever take place. Indeed, no new developments should be undertaken at all until the existing buildings are fully used and the decay has been arrested. Even then, the only alteration to the fabric should be in the nature of repair and enhancement rather than wholesale surgery or grafting. Trees will have to be planted to replace those reaching the end of their lives, and unsightly holes in walls or in the structure should be filled using local materials. Here is where a store of stone for walling and roofing is an absolutely essential ingredient in the future conservation of Oxfordshire villages.

A rise in village population will not revive farms nor will it bring life back to the village in its traditional form.[7] All that an increase in housing of the type and numbers suggested in the report would have done was to increase the numbers of commuters with a resultant effect on the community. This increase would have meant more cars. More cars would have created reasons for widening the roads with resultant loss of the small-scale enclosed character of Wytham. More traffic, wider roads, and more people would have brought about paved footpaths, street lights, standard concrete kerbs, parking lots, garages, noise, and all the things associated with a motorised population. In no time at all, no matter how reasonable and well-intentioned the proposals might seem, Wytham would have become suburbanised, with sight-lines, glare, harsh edges to the roads, and the paraphernalia associated with numbers of cars and a lot of people.

The traffic-generating power of the Wytham pub is considerable, and its visual effect cannot be ignored. The Trout at Godstow is another instance where the cars take up an area several times greater than that occupied by the pub. There can be little doubt that when Mr. ffennell made his gesture in the 'forties, he could hardly have foreseen the immense growth of private ownership of the motor-car. Yet Mr. ffennell's directions are quite clear. In his pamphlet, *Oxford as it was, now is and never should be*, he demonstrated his hatred of ugliness and the destruction of beauty and peace. He was determined to 'secure the preservation of the estate with its great natural beauty for all future time'. Motor-cars and considerable development would hardly contribute to this 'security'. On the contrary, Wytham's character would be in mortal danger if any major development were to be carried out, and its qualities are being eroded now by the influx of motor traffic alone.

Wytham possesses a degree of organic integrity due mostly to its construction of local materials. Large trees, clusters of small-scale buildings and their harmonious lines, all contribute to the charms of the environment. Part of the village is dilapidated. Much could be restored and enhanced. New planting, much conversion, and a great deal of screening by means of walls and trees could work wonders in the village.

The subtle qualities and gentle, unobtrusive, simple dignity of a vernacular architecture with its roots in the soil of Oxfordshire could be destroyed if ever major new developments were to proceed. Housing clusters such as those proposed in the report could not be said to complement the existing village.

Wytham needs careful nursing. It needs surgery and setting, repair and restoration, planting for posterity, the treating of several wounds, and general conservation and enhancement. It must be protected from 'infill' on any scale, and it could not survive a greatly increased number of people, houses, or cars.

When re-use of existing housing stock is increasingly regarded as a national priority, fabric as fine as that in Wytham should offer scope. Linch Farm has already been converted. In 1969 it seemed that the plans proposed in the report *Wytham: How to save the village*, were approved by the various bodies concerned. The Oxford Civic Society, and many other private individuals, however, asked if the proposals conflicted with the terms and conditions of the original Deed of Agreement into which Mr. ffennell entered with the University. If the proposals conflicted, and if the University proceeded with such a development, it was argued, it became clear that there was a serious danger that the intentions of the grantor would have been betrayed. It became clear that, if there was a conflict, bodies which supported the development were helping to betray the trust which Mr. ffennell so nobly placed in the 'kindly sympathy' of the University. In 1970 it was not too late to reconsider all the issues involved, nor would it have been ignoble or a sign of weakness to go over a policy before implementation. The University was entrusted with part of the heritage of Oxford and its surroundings by a man who loved that heritage and desired never to see it destroyed. I was asked to write a piece on Wytham for *Oxford*, the magazine of the Oxford Society, in 1970. In that article I stated that a *'great and kindly act of beneficence which was expressly made to preserve Wytham must not be betrayed, nor must a decision be made in good faith which would have the effect of betraying that trust'*. I further expressed the hope that the dangers would be realised before the damage was done, and that Wytham would remain for ever as Mr. ffennell hoped it would. The previous November[8] an article was carried by the *Oxford Mail* which argued the conservation case, and showed large numbers of views of the village. So far, the messages of the articles, and the opinions expressed, appear to have had the effect desired. There have been further signs of erosion in Wytham, but the drastic changes proposed in 1969 have not taken place. It is my fervent hope they never will. If Mr. ffennell's trust is betrayed, then truly it can be said that *Tempora mutantur nos et mutamur in illis. Quomodo? Fit semper tempore pejor homo.*

[1] *Wytham.* A record issued by the Oxford Preservation Trust on the Acquisition of Wytham Abbey and Estate by the University of Oxford. 1943. p. 3.
[2] Ibid. p. 3
[3] Ibid. p. 5
[4] Ibid. p. 5
[5] Ibid. p. 5
[6] Ibid. p. 6
[7] 'The Changing Village'. Article in *Official Architecture and Planning* by James Stevens Curl. November, 1971.
[8] 'Wytham — a village in danger'. Article by Adytum in the *Oxford Mail,* 19 November 1969.

Epilogue

'The photographer is a historian in
himself — a historian who makes no
mistakes, who has no prejudices,
but who registers things just as he
finds them.'

A discussion of the work of the
famous Oxford photographer,
Henry W. Taunt, in the *Oxford
Chronicle,* 21 September 1911

Oxford is many things to many men. The great upsurge of activity in the Church of England in the first half of the nineteenth century gave tremendous stimulus to the phenomenal amount of church-building in Victoria's reign, while the Catholic element of the Oxford Movement gave impetus to the Gothic Revival. The defection of Newman and others caused a turmoil, and Oxford was described as 'The Half-Way House to Rome'.[1] Sir Max Beerbohm in *Going Back to School* said that it was Oxford that had made him 'insufferable', and Edward Gibbon, in his *Autobiography*, wrote:

To the University of Oxford I acknowledge no obligation; and she will as cheerfully renounce me for a son, as I am willing to disclaim her for a mother. I spent fourteen months at Magdalen College: they proved the fourteen months the most idle and unprofitable of my whole life.

The mystique, the charm, and the reputation of Oxford, however, have been potent for many generations.

Oxford to him a dearer name shall be, Than his own mother University

declared John Dryden in his *Prologue to the University of Oxford*. It would be a strange man or woman who, having lived in the city of Oxford for however short a time, did not respond to its spell.

It is painful to see many of the changes that have occurred in Oxford. It is even more painful to contemplate what very nearly happened only a few years ago.

Oxford City Council had proposed an amended development plan which was largely the remains of the Development Plan Review grafted on to Scheme D of the Consultants' Report. This was largely the result of the then Minister's advice following the Review Inquiry that since he 'was not prepared to give effect to the proposals for the principal traffic routes', but accepted part of the Review, despite the recommendation of the Inspector to the contrary, Consultants were to be appointed to advise on road and traffic schemes.

The result was the Amendment 2, 1970, which left Oxford's problems unsolved but would have involved Oxford's citizens in huge increases in rates.

An examination of the present transport methods in Oxford reveals the astounding fact that road and rail are not properly integrated nor would they be if the Plan were implemented. Clearly, the key to any successful transport policy must be the rationalisation of all forms of transport, and if the bus station is not physically and administratively linked with rail, water and private transport, then chaos must result. Oxford's station needs a physical and administrative link with the bus station. The logical centre for development as a transportation heart is therefore the site of the present station, and here a new bus station and water bus station at Osney Town could provide the core of an efficient public transport network.

Oxford's river is neglected and underused. There is an ideal water route for fast buses on the river and on the canal. A terminus at Osney Town, on the East bank of the river, linked to a complex of railway and bus terminus buildings as well as car parks and taxi ranks, pedestrian routes to Oxford and bicycle paths could provide the most advanced and successful public transport service in Britain. A relief Road exists. It is called the ring road, and it is underused. All that is needed is a

194

spur connection from the by-pass to the Station Complex, and a huge amount of traffic normally carried on the Botley, Abingdon, Woodstock, Banbury, Iffley, Cowley and Headington Roads would be reduced. Enforced use of the by-pass and the attractions of local rail traffic as well as water buses would improve matters beyond recognition, while public transport *properly managed and directed and integrated* would reduce the present desire (and in some cases necessity) to use the private car in Oxford.

The question will be asked concerning East Oxford. I answer this by pointing out that river buses and an efficient bus service would take much of the existing pressure off the roads, while diversion along the by-pass would prevent Magdalen Bridge being used for traffic as at present. If the spur link from the west were to be taken *south* of Osney Town so as to serve the industrial estate as well, and if it were then to connect with the station complex *and* with an improved Donnington Bridge Road, the East Oxford and High Street would have the relief they need. The point is this: the Council's plans for Donnington Bridge were out of date when they were implemented. Transport must be looked at as a whole, and not as little isolated problems. Road, rail, the private car, the river, the canal, pedestrian routes and all modes of getting about must be seen as being inter-related: they are *not* to be considered in isolation.

Our towns are faced with the biggest threat ever to their structure, their institutions, and their very being. Oxford is no exception, The roads lobby, which is perhaps the strongest government has ever faced, would have us believe that the answer to overcrowded roads, traffic jams and urban chaos is to build more roads and bigger roads. Fiscal policy on capital is likely to destroy much of the fabric of towns, while making it uneconomic to look after old buildings. Thinking is so muddled on these points that it is clear the most elementary blunders are being made in dealing with the problems of traffic in towns, and thinking seems to be dominated by theories and models of reality which are seen to be destructive and useless, yet we persist.

Anyone who doubts that traffic in towns is destructive should look at twilight areas of any city in the British Isles, or even closer to home, the by-pass, St. Ebbe's, Botley Road, Hythe Bridge Street. It is not the old buildings, the mixture of activities, the structure or anything of that nature which is so awful. It is the anarchy of traffic and all that entails, including road signs, lights, painted lines, smell and noise which appals; it is the chaos and intrusion of traffic into areas where people live; it is the destruction and erosion of the visual, physical, useful environment of thousands and thousands of people which is so frightening. Cities and towns were never built for the vast incursions of millions of private motor cars, with their noise, danger, smells, and sheer numbers.

We must make our decision. We must ask ourselves if we *want* to get into the position of having to destroy large areas of our city in order to allow the motor car easier access; if we want our revenue-producing areas taken up with non-revenue producing roads and our parks; if we want to see whole communities, houses, streets, replaced with windswept wildernesses of tarmac for the use of the private motor car; if we want a civilised environment, or a miniature Los Angeles.

Let us face the facts. Lower-paid workers who cannot afford to run a car have to use public transport. They are subsidising the system which is being strangled by those who can afford to do without it. The streams of cars pouring into Oxford daily from the outlying villages and the suburbs with only one person per car will be a familiar sight to many. It *cannot* make sense. Public transport in Oxford is not as good as it ought to be because among other things, during rush hours, it cannot function properly because of the congestion caused by the private motor car.

Estimates for road building in this country vary. The dreadful reality of American experience has demonstrated:

1. Increased road use demand quickly renders new urban motorways inadequate.
2. Urban disturbance, both physical and social, is of an unparalleled extent where the motor car is catered for.
3. The grim environment which is essentially due to the new scale demanded by the motor vehicle is non-human and alien to mankind.
4. Public transport goes out of business because the car is subsidised by the taxpayer and the user of the private car does not pay enough for bringing his car into urban areas. Many American municipalities are facing a total breakdown of public services because they are bankrupting themselves in order to cater for the folly of bringing cars far into the centres of towns. We all know how much room cars need in car parks and on the roads. Huge acreages of car parks in the centre of Oxford, besides being visually hideous, preventing the physical structure necessary for a social community to develop, and causing noise and danger in order to get to the centre, cannot make sense. It presents gross waste.

It is the principle which must be looked at. Always, it has been assumed that we *must* have a relief road because the traffic in Oxford is considerable. If we do not permit the traffic to enter the town, we do not need an 'inner relief road'; we do not need to destroy anything of the city; and St. Ebbe's could be rebuilt for people to live there instead of out in Blackbird Leys and other places which must entail a transport problem. In order to cater for the motor car in the city we should have to destroy a great deal. This is terrible in terms of human misery and uprooting. If we amputate, carve and penetrate the structure of the city in the way proposed by the road lobby, we end up with such destruction that we approach a wilderness. There is no point in having an operation when the patient dies.

It is amazing to consider that any body or individual if faced with expenditure on the scale proposed by the City five years ago would undoubtedly carry out experiments to see what the other possibilities were. The Council proposed to commit itself and the inhabitants of Oxford to a grandiose scheme on the flimsiest of pretexts and without any genuine attempt to carry out proper experiment. This is irresponsible, for just because local government has enormous power (especially in planning matters), there can be no excuse for abusing that power. No decision should be made until proper experimentation in traffic management and public transport has been carried out. No attempt was made to manage the traffic in such a way that the construction of huge car parks and roads would be unnecessary.

No effort had gone into providing an efficient and workable public transport system where all modes of transport would be integrated. The present railway station is unrelated to the bus station; the river and canal are almost totally ignored, yet they are ideal links for water buses and for heavy transport; the present bus service is poor; and transport generally is left in its little and varied compartments with no attempt to unite and rationalise the various modes of transport. There is no point in building a massive road system which peters out at the bottom of Headington Hill and which destroys without solving anything much. The only road system which could work is that based on the existing by-pass, which is under-used, with a spur *south* of Osney Town to take traffic to and past the industrial estate there, with a connection via the Oxpens to a new transport complex at the railway station embracing buses, trains, and water transport. Osney Town and St. Thomas's must be linked for pedestrians only: whatever happens these oases must not be wrecked by the road juggernaut.

The Oxford Civic Society produced a brief but readable booklet in response to the Council's turgid documents. This was called appropriately *Let's LIVE in Oxford*. It examined and exposed the Council's plans in simple terms so that the layman did not have to wade through the undigested tedium of deadly prose. Above all, the pamphlet of the Society argued that *social costs*, totally ignored by the Council, should be added to the capital sum involved in destroying communities and replacing them with monuments to the private motor car and to municipal wrong-headedness. *People* count, argued the Society, and their communities and social structures should not be disrupted for such specious reasons.

The Chairman of Oxford City Finance Committee is reported as saying (*Oxford Mail*, 2 June 1970) that it had cost £300,000 in *administrative* costs in connection with the road plans. The age of the Caesars is not over. Demagogues are always ready to push through any scheme which is grand and expensive enough in order to further something (usually ambitious) other than good planning and the creation of pleasant environment. Local Government exists as the servant of the electorate. It exists to ensure that certain essential services are provided and maintained by employees, who are answerable to the Council, who are in turn answerable to the electorate. These services include good planning, which should involve the organising of building and land use in pursuance of an express scheme of urban or rural evolution. Muddle, ugliness, destruction and the ruination of the existing environment will not achieve these aims. If the then Council had carried out its plan it would have meant a severe mutilation of Oxford and its communities. The electorate was concerned that its servants appeared to consider themselves the masters.

Fortunately, the public debate that had been stimulated caused several new elections to the Council. A change of party brought in the beginnings of experiment. Bus lanes, more restriction of the private car, and some pedestrianisation began the experiment. It was a minor start, but it *was* a start.

It is to be hoped that never again will there be destruction on the scale of Tudor times or the 'redevelopment' of St. Ebbe's, where there has been precious little 'development' but a lot of destruction. Oxford is too valuable to damage any more. Let us have a final look at some

Fig. 1: Merton Street, part of the essential Oxford

of the lessons which could be learned from the past.

Merton Street, like so many parts of Oxford, offers something of the essence of Oxford's spell (fig. 1). The great chapel of Merton stands sentinel over the street, while other less pretentious buildings set off the grander edifices.

Peckwater Quad, in Christ Church, was laid out by Henry Aldrich between 1705 and 1714, and the classical correctness of the buildings contrast with the massive Baroque of Clark's Library (fig. 2). In Peckwater, a standard Oxford enclosure is found, as in Radcliffe Square, with a massive building set off by smaller, less overpowering elements, so that the eye is led onwards to new delights. Beyond is the tower of Merton, and a plain triumphal arch.

Left: fig. 2 Part of Peckwater Quad, Christ Church, looking east into Canterbury Quad past the huge Baroque library (right).

Right: fig. 3 Looking into Canterbury Quad, showing the triumphal arch of Wyatt. The inscription commemorates Richard Robinson, Archbishop of Armagh, the Church of Ireland Primate of the eighteenth century, who was also the patron of the celebrated Irish architect, Francis Johnston. Note the scale of the huge Baroque library on the right.

In entering Canterbury Quad the scale is again different. The Quad was built in 1773—83 by Wyatt at the expense of Richard Robinson, Archbishop of Armagh, Church of Ireland Primate. The elegant arch, the corner lamps, and simple Georgian detail combine in a pleasing composition, yet the beholder is always enticed to explore further (fig. 3).

Other delights were provided by the designers of the cloisters at New College. The single-frame pointed wagon roof is probably one of the finest in Britain, and the cloisters are a place of infinite peace (fig. 4). More open, and less picturesque are the cloisters of Magdalen College, yet the lessons of enclosure, of human scale, and of intimate spaces are still apparent (fig. 5).

Oxford is a city where views are nearly always framed, so that the eye is constantly being led from one space to another. Corpus and Christ Church both offer many examples of archways with spaces and quads beyond (fig. 6).

Fig. 4: New College Cloisters

Other principles are frequently found, including the positive architectural statement in a space, of which the Radcliffe Camera must be the finest example. The old Grammar Hall at Magdalen College of the seventeenth century, complete with its bell-tower, is another example (fig. 7), while the former Chemistry Laboratory (based on the Abbot's Kitchen at Glastonbury and designed by Benjamin Woodward, of Sir Thomas Deane, Son, and Woodward of Dublin) formerly obeyed the same principle, though it has now been connected up to other buildings by many late additions (fig. 8). The latter is adjacent to the University Museum.

Durham Quad in Trinity College again shows us enclosure in another dress. Fig. 9 shows the north range by William Townesend, of 1728. The alleyway is even smaller and more mysterious than is usual in Oxford. Townesend also was involved in the erection of the New Buildings of Magdalen with Dr. Clarke in 1733. The palatial façade is another self-contained statement set this time in an Arcadian landscape rather than in an urban matrix (fig. 10). Strong elements like New Buildings hold the eye, and fix a visual point in space. The same principle is found in Headington, where a group of houses terminates a vista and provides a strong enough element to enclose the end of a street (fig. 11).

Elsewhere in this book I have discussed those objects that make up the urban fabric, not only buildings and roads, but trees, walls, railings, lamps, water, and countless details that combine to form the whole. I have emphasised that almost daily changes are taking place

Above: fig. 5 Magdalen College cloisters

Below: fig. 6 Enclosure, framing and enticement at Christ Church

Below right: fig. 7 An object in space: the Grammar Hall at Magdalen

Above: fig. 8 Another positive architectural statement, this time the chemical laboratory based on the Abbot's Kitchen at Glastonbury, and designed by Benjamen Woodward in Victorian times.

Left: fig. 9 Durham Quad, Trinity

Below: fig. 10 New Buildings, Magdalen

that are essentially ruinous to the quality of our urban environment.

The replacement of the old lamps, for example, unobtrusively fixed as they once were to the walls of buildings, is a major source of disquiet. The modern designs are geared to mass production and so are not made of those materials which married in with the structure of towns in the past, such as cast iron and copper, with wrought iron brackets or cast-iron standards. New lamps tend not to be fixed to walls, but are placed on slender posts of thin metal which proliferate the clutter of the contemporary scene while looking quite wrong. It is not a question of arguments about costs, but of whether or not the material *feels* right in the context of an urban environment. Cast iron *is* a good material, and has been proved to last for a very long time. In the Oxford townscape of mellow stone, carved wood and soft plastered walls, the new lamps look out of place, and their inherent ugliness is magnified. The bankruptcy of sensibility which threatens Oxford is the antithesis of what remains of fine townscape. The buildings that make up the historic core are in possession of that inner repose which has its being in that moment of purpose which created them. The spiritual emptiness of much of what is being done to Oxford's physical fabric is born of expediency. Its influence is everywhere to be seen, eating away the legacies of finer ages like a cancer, out of shame, ignorance or envy.

Wholesale demolition has done great damage. St. Ebbe's and the erosion of Cornmarket and Longwall come to mind. Countless details that delight the eye can disappear overnight. One or two items might hardly be missed, but when all the details vanish, a bareness and loss of human interest, of the craftsman's touch, result.

An outdoor seat in a porch in a pub at Marston was a charming feature (fig. 12). The bootscraper and worn stone step spoke eloquently of a well-loved place. A crucifix, shaded by churchyard trees in St. Thomas's adds a curiously Gallic touch to this part of Oxford (fig. 13). Details such as these add infinitely to character.

The power held by local authorities is enormous. We must never forget that it is the holders of political power who determine the environment. Once it was the Church, then it was the Nation-State, then it was the commercial powers. Now it is local and central government. The logical outcome of a Nazi regime was the environment of an Auschwitz and total destruction. The architecture of monasticism and mediaeval society reflects the enclosure, the tightly-knit community dominated by the Church and its institutions. The environment of today reflects the abysmal mediocrity of the power-groups and individuals who make decisions affecting our surroundings. The physical aspects of our cities reflect our own level of civilisation. The kind of thing we are now used to expect are: lamps of incredible ugliness; wasted space of awful appearance; buildings of inelegance; the townscape of despair; the waste land; the physical expression of spiritual, moral and creative collapse. In such an environment there can be no pleasure, no redeeming feature, no hope. We must not forget that erosion is the direct creation of those very powers and individuals who are entrusted with the remoulding of Oxford and the making of new urban structures which we will have to live with for a long and unappetising time. Compared with the environments of the past it is doubtful if we can be happy at the prospect before us. It is equally doubtful if we can

Fig. 11: A visual 'stop' at Old Headington

trust the decision-makers to produce anything of the quality of Oxford past.

    With all these lessons, with the tremendous background of intellect and sensibility, you would imagine that Oxford in the twentieth century could have met the challenge and come up with a better record than it has. You would also imagine that, given its wonderful setting of hills, woods and rivers, it would have been careful to conserve the assets that it had. You might have thought, realistically too, that Oxford would have done a better job to house and employ those who work in the ancient centre or who earn their living in the new industrial areas.

    Oxford has failed, as have most other towns in these islands. The people of these lands were once possessed of the creative force. That force was once very strong in Oxford. It is perhaps worth speculating as to what has become of it. The answer lies in several factors. The first is that the political system badly needs overhauling, for political decisions affect the physical environment, but the most important is that there is no philosophy based on aesthetic and spiritual values which can balance the purely expedient and empirical arguments which are used to make decisions. Until a way can be found where spiritual, economic, aesthetic, physical, political, empirical, and artistic forces unite, there can be little hope for Oxford. The empirical spell, which demands a measure to be placed on everything before it can be evaluated, must be broken. Architecture does not depend upon purely empirical values for its excellence, for much of the vernacular architecture of Oxford has no discernible system of measurement which is responsible for its character, nor can any financial value be

Left: fig. 12   A pub porch at Marston, now altered

Right: fig. 13   A crucifix at St. Thomas's

given which can adequately describe it. Empiricism ignores the un-measurable, and any attempt to evaluate the urban environment by applying a systems approach is bound to give the wrong answer.

The lessons of human scale, of enclosure, of emphasis, of quality in townscape, or sensitivity in the use of materials are all found in Oxford. All the lessons of how to destroy those assets can also be found here. We ignore the warnings at our peril, and if we give *carte blanche* to those forces which have amply demonstrated their inability to create an environment of any decency, we have only ourselves to blame.

Until a way can be found where spiritual, economic, aesthetic, physical and vernacular-traditional forces unite, there can be no hope for our environment, in Oxford or anywhere else. Until we have a national renaissance based on the eternal verities of beauty found in the real Oxford, on a regional, national and *international* scale, we cannot resolve anything, even at a local level.

It is this lack of national direction, this lack of identity which, I suggest contributes to the Erosion of Oxford, and is mirrored in the destruction around us.

[1] Punch, Vol. XVI, 1849, p.36.

'When the High Lama asked him whether Shangri-la was not unique in his experience, and if the Western world could offer anything in the least like it, he answered with a smile: "Well, yes — to be quite frank, it reminds me very slightly of Oxford".'

James Hilton: *Lost Horizon,* Ch. 9